HQ
759.64
.P46
1987

Pennetti, Michael.

Coping with
schoolage
fatherhood

$12.95

DATE			
MAR. 1988			

© THE BAKER & TAYLOR CO.

COPING WITH

School Age Fatherhood

Michael Pennetti

THE ROSEN PUBLISHING GROUP, INC. NEW YORK

Published in 1987, 1988 by The Rosen Publishing Group, Inc.
29 East 21st Street, New York NY 10010

REVISED EDITION 1988

Library of Congress Cataloging-in-Publication Data

Pennetti, Michael.
  Coping with schoolage fatherhood.

  Bibliography: p.
  Includes index.
  1. Adolescent fathers—United States.
2. Teen-age marriage—United States. 3. Youth—
United States—Sexual behavior. I. Title.
HQ759.64.P46 1987   306.8'1'088055   86-20288
ISBN 0-8239-0824-0

Manufactured in the United States of America

To my parents, my wife, Susan,
my sons Michael and Christopher,
and my best friend Alan.

Contents

Preface

n the fall of 1981 I walked down the aisle in my wedding ceremony to an unknown and terrifying future. I was in the middle of my second year in junior college, with $542 in the bank and a baby due in six months. For someone who knew as little about the "real world" as I did, the next thirty-six months were to be both a terrific and a frightening experience. It is not a period that I would like to repeat, but the lessons I learned could not be bought at any price.

Today I have a bachelor's degree, a managerial position, and a caring wife and two sons to show for my efforts. Regardless of pessimistic predictions, a teenage father's fight can be won.

Introduction

One of the most troubling and yet influential periods of a person's life is adolescence. In our society, adolescence may be considered to have three stages: early, middle, and late. Most acute in this decade of incessant turmoil are the years between the ages of sixteen and nineteen. They are a period of rapid biological and physical changes, developing self-concepts and social values, changing interpersonal relationships and styles of thought, and emerging sexuality patterns. All this is condensed into barely four years of time. The young person is faced with tremendous pressures both from within and from society as a whole. Is it really such a wonder under the circumstances that our teenagers are viewed as confused and disturbed?

The cure for the ills of adolescence is, of course, adulthood. But for a growing percentage of our teenage population adulthood comes earlier than expected. As a consequence of the sexual revolution, the rate of adolescents having babies has more than tripled in the years from 1940 to 1980. The sexual freedom has been accompanied by failure to use birth control measures, through either ignorance or unwillingness to accept responsibility. Some 550,000 babies are born each year to teenage mothers, according to the National Center for Health Statistics. Statistics show that less than half of the teenage fathers remain to support their new family, but on the brighter side, the same figures mean that nearly half do stay to raise a family. Some do an excellent job in helping their children to grow while themselves continuing to develop toward adulthood. However, assistance is almost always necessary for this to be accomplished.

Helping a young couple with a child is helping to secure society's own future. That correlation is simple and straightforward but seldom appreciated. My contribution to that cause is the offer of experience, knowledge, facts, and advice to one member of the young family unit—the teenage father. To a young father struggling with his own life and the life of his family, this book may or may not be helpful. But to one who has the courage to accept responsibility and gains the wisdom to cope with it, I would say he has already begun to turn the odds in his favor.

P A R T ◇ 1

CHAPTER 1

Choices and Chances

First, congratulations are in order on your achievement. Many men are incapable of fathering a child naturally and must turn to recently developed and still rather expensive medical technology. However, you are now a teenage father or father-to-be, and most people, including yourself, are reluctant to accept the situation as anything but sheer disaster. Fortunately, that viewpoint does not last long, thanks to the fact that people's memory tends to be as short as their temper. That may not be very reassuring at the moment, but remember that inside every nervous parent is a patient grandparent looking forward to a child from his own offspring someday. It applies to your parents as well as yourself, even though the day may have come sooner than expected.

If you have not yet told your parents the news, remember that a woman's pregnancy is not like a rash that will go away. Ignoring the difficulties will not make them disappear. The time to tell them is now. Avoiding the issue does not make the situation any simpler or easier later when they are inevitably confronted with the facts.

It is less painful for all involved if the parents are informed promptly with honesty and consideration. Hopefully, they will respond the same way. Yes, the news will hurt your parents and shock your friends. But no, the pain is not permanent, and the chances are that your current friends and acquaintances will not be part of your life for much longer anyway. You will soon go your separate ways and have nothing in common besides age and the school you attended.

Your parents are quite a different matter. They can offer emotional and possibly financial support at a time when it is most needed in your life to make a clear judgment on the many decisions you now face. Listen to their guidance and advice. Now, as always, they are only trying to do what is in your best interest. Although perhaps not starting out as early as you have, they themselves have certainly been where you are now headed, toward being a parent. Only someone in that position can really understand and appreciate what it means. A child that is *your* son or daughter is on its way into the world. For good or ill, this is the only world we have, and the people coming into it must be well taught and cared for if it is to get any better. That is your responsibility as a parent and a father in particular.

Father is not a title to be taken lightly; throughout their entire lives your children will have only one true father—you. Teenage or not, your duties will include guardian, role model, engineer, protector, psychologist, therapist, provider, playmate, judge, coach, banker, medic, lawyer, and so on. Nearly every job on an occupational list will be attempted at one time or another by a father.

The extent of the influence a father exerts on his children is determined by many factors, but most important are how closely he observes their upbringing and how attentive he is to their needs. By this I mean the living arrangements of the family.

One of the first decisions a teenage father must make after accepting responsibility for his new family is the nature of the relationship itself. Three choices are inherent in the structure of the household, each involving a different degree of family unity and intimacy. From the least to the most tightly bonded are living apart, living together (cohabitation), and marriage. The sexual revolution of the 1960s and 1970s has greatly reduced the social bias against the first two but still adamantly encourages the third.

Circumstances will naturally affect the life-style that is chosen, but personal outlooks and opinions tend to change with experience. Therefore, all three may be adopted over a period of time. For example, a couple may begin their relationship living together with no legal commitment and decide later to marry. Or, conversely, they may marry and later obtain a marital separation. Whichever path is chosen, the fact is that only one can be taken initially.

First mentioned is the arrangement of living apart, in which a father assumes financial responsibility but has little if any contact with his new family. Emotionally, it is the least restrictive of the three choices of life-styles. It is well adapted for the father who wishes to care for his family without actually having a family. No legal documentation is involved; it is basically a verbal agreement between the parties.

Living apart is also the least rewarding alternative, since little satisfaction can be gained through watching from a distance the growth and development of the child. The father is not a part of the family he is helping to support and is soon reduced to being merely an additional source of income or a kind of preemptive child support. The mother and child may become for him only another payment, like buying a car or a television set. It is not surprising that this type of relationship is short-lived at best in the vast majority of cases. Gradually, visits to the family go from occasional to rare to non-existent, and the support payments usually follow the same downward pattern.

In some cases this pattern may be an outgrowth of government regulations concerning welfare and other aid payments for dependent children. When the father is present in the household, the family usually can expect no benefits or assistance of any type. Once again bureaucracy becomes an ugly word.

The second option to be considered is cohabitation, or living with the mother and child with no legal agreement or ties. Social resistance to this type of relationship is lessening but still exists, especially among the pre-1960s generation, who contemptuously called it "shacking up." The birth of a child may emphasize this position, as the couple's parents may pressure their children to make a traditional marriage for the sake of permanence.

Cohabitation may or may not be similar to marriage depending on the relationship and the individual personalities of the couple. It is often characterized by a relatively open acknowledgment between the partners that they are not in a state of being married. Living together thus excludes the advantage of clearly defined roles and expectations inherent in marriage. It does, however, offer greater freedom for the partners to design and adapt their roles to fit their particular circumstances in a way they feel is most beneficial and rewarding for themselves.

Couples who are living together must also face many sociological problems that are not basic to the relationship itself. For example, informing one's parents of the decision to live with a person of the opposite sex usually takes a knack of diplomacy. Many couples try to ease the impact of the announcement by dropping subtle hints and clues that are difficult to ignore. This method can reduce the initial surprise of the news but tends to prolong what could be a rather tense situation. "Hi Dad, the Cubs won today, I'm moving in with my girlfriend who's pregnant, I hope they win again tomorrow," doesn't really qualify as subtle.

Also, couples often have trouble finding a suitable title for the partner. It's easy to put Mr. John Smith and Miss Sally Jones on the mailbox, but how would you refer to the other person when in the company of friends or family? "Girlfriend," "roommate," "friend," and "lover" all seem somewhat inadequate. The problem is likewise faced by those who wish to send the couple a Christmas card, an invitation, or other joint correspondence. Eloquence, charm, tact, and a good imagination are definitely helpful qualities in this case.

On a different note, financial considerations may crop up. Although the father is living with and supporting his family, without the legal evidence of a marriage certificate he cannot claim them as dependents. He is thus deprived of many insurance and tax reductions.

Finally, social double standards represent a particularly common nuisance for a couple living together. As was demonstrated by the popular TV situation comedy

"Three's Company," it may enhance a man's personal image to be living with a woman, but it is usually detrimental to a woman's stature and reputation to be living with a man. The actual or implied sexual nature of cohabitation can be especially harmful among professional colleagues, again being most damaging among women. Between the couple, commitment is a matter of overriding concern to be handled through prior arrangement, especially as regards a child. Family permanence is essential for the growth and development of children and, to a large extent, their parents. A stable environment permits building and planning the future. The interests of the child must be balanced with those of the parents. For a teenage father, family permanence is a valuable asset that may help to alleviate the problems and stresses of sudden parenthood. Its practical benefits should not be either underrated or overlooked. Building on firm ground makes any structure stronger, including a family.

Accurate statistics on cohabitation are difficult to compile. Couples are reluctant to announce their relationship to a researcher for fear of social rejection or prejudice. Also, the temporary nature of the life-style complicates record-keeping. If a couple no longer reside at the same address over the space of a year, as is often the case, it could be attributed to their moving elsewhere, splitting up, or getting married. We usually don't know which.

As best as can be determined for the population as a whole, cohabitation more than doubled during the 1970s. The life-style seems to be especially attractive to people under the age of twenty-five, as their frequency of living together increased eightfold in that period. Over 25 percent of the households had children. For those who consider living together as a sort of fashionable trial run before marriage, it should be noted that only about 30 percent of couples living together eventually marry. The percentage is only slightly higher for those with children.

By far the most popular choice of teenage fathers wanting to care for their new family is marriage. The overwhelming majority of American men, teenage or not, eventually marry at least once. The proportion was put at 93 percent by the 1980 Census.

Saying goodbye to single life, for better or for worse, is something hundreds of thousands of people do each year, and for many it is not to be the first or the last time. That fact implies that, despite the high divorce rate, there is still something rare and worthwhile in a successful marriage that impels people to repeatedly take the harsh emotional and financial risks involved in such a venture. Nearly 80 percent of all divorced people remarry. A happy marriage and the raising of a family offer rewards that are unique: pride, companionship, security, love, respect, fulfillment, happiness, and personal growth, to name a few. All the money in the world could not purchase those values. Ever wonder why so many movie stars and famous personalities marry so often in their careers? Listen to the old Beatles' tune "Money Can't Buy Me Love" and I think you'll know the answer.

Parents naturally want to see their children obtain those same valuable benefits. Understand that when you feel pressured and plagued by parents to marry. Putting aside all the talk of what's morally or socially right, if there is such a thing, they see an opportunity for you to gain something priceless. They have no power to endow you with it, but they can steer you in the right direction. A child born to a happy couple, no matter what their ages, can bring a lot of love into a lot of lives. Two people loving and cooperating to rear a third is a wonderful experience, in spite of the many inconveniences involved in caring for a baby. Love, after all, is what marriage is all about, and it is the one ingredient that makes possible the possession of true happiness in a relationship.

Of course, success is ultimately up to you and your partner. Constant and clear communication and cooperation are vital features of a healthy and thriving relationship. Both are difficult to maintain, but without them there is no basis for even the most shallow bond between two people, two companies, or two nations.

To decide between the life-styles presented in this chapter also requires communication and cooperation. The choice may be the first of many major decisions you will be required to make in life, although none may ever be quite as serious or important. Don't shut off the world or the caring people around you who can help to lessen the burden of sudden adulthood. Yesterday you were a boy, and today you're a man. As much as you may wish otherwise, and be assured there will be many times, you will be a man from now until the last day of your life. That is a fact of life that cannot be changed. People grow up. To view facts in a responsible and practical manner in order to reach the best decision is an inescapable consequence of adulthood, but it need not be done alone. Don't neglect the advantage of advice from parents, relatives, friends, peers, and soon quite possibly a wife.

To do so would be foolish and damaging in the long run. With all the immediate choices and chances facing him, a teenager above all else cannot afford to be a fool.

CHAPTER 2

I Do, I Will

I remember the very first time I faced the thought of getting married. Disregarding a formal proposal, which seemed rather unnecessary under the circumstances, we had decided to marry as soon as possible. Again considering the situation, our parents took the news solemnly but rather well. The countdown to the baby's estimated arrival was at T minus seven months.

We avoided the potential complications inherent in the fact that our families belong to different religious denominations by consenting to wed in a backyard ritual by a justice of the peace. It wasn't exactly how I had always pictured my wedding, but a major family feud was handily averted.

I sat one evening watching television as my future wife and in-laws discussed the final preparations for the ceremony, which was now hardly ten days away. Suddenly, as if someone had turned on a bright light in a dark room, I realized that it was actually *I* that they were talking about. I listened, or eavesdropped depending on the point of view, for a few moments as they discussed where I was supposed to stand, how I was to enter and exit, and other such details. For weeks it had been as if I were participating in the arrangements for someone else's wedding. Now I knew inside that it was really mine. My usual reserve and calmness left me as quickly as if I were sitting in the path of an oncoming freight train. I had heard about having second thoughts or "cold feet" before one's wedding, but I was frozen from head to toe. To say I was scared is an understatement comparable to calling Beverly Hills a middle-class neighborhood. I continued to watch television, but now with an almost hypnotic attention. A skit was in progress on the "Carol Burnett Show" in which Harvey Korman and Tim Conway comically slapped around a small hand puppet; somehow I knew how that puppet must have felt. I later discovered that what I had experienced was actually a mild form of shock reaction. In any case, when the conversation turned to looking for apartments and comparing prices, I thought it was a good time to leave.

It should be noted that at the time I had a total of $542.43 in the bank and a job that paid the royal salary of $82 per week. Not bad for a second-year college student living at home, but hardly adequate for one wanting to support and house a family. That was especially true considering that rents for decent apartments started at $300 a month plus first and last months and a security deposit. Needless to say, we decided more out of necessity than choice to stay with my parents for a while after we were married.

Continuing to use my own case as an example, let's review the situation for a moment. The hindering factors involved are a severely limited income, unfinished schooling, lack of adequate and affordable housing, and last but certainly not least, an overwhelming (but understandable) feeling of insecurity and loss of self-confidence. In many ways that last component is the most serious problem if it lasts for any unusually long period.

It is an accepted fact that some people naturally regain their composure faster than others. Self-confidence and personal security reinforce the will to survive and the desire to forge ahead that are as vital to your progress as water to a running stream. Make no mistake, what you're entangled in is a struggle: the struggle of life. That becomes especially clear during the first year, which is usually the most difficult because of adjustment problems. But you have effective tools and weapons at your disposal in the struggle.

First and foremost among those tools are organizational skills. You will soon notice that imperceptibly your world has begun to shrink. People you used to see, places you used to visit, and interests you used to have will all be considerably lessened or totally discarded. That is undoubtedly healthy, because a limited environment can be more easily evaluated and understood. You are setting priorities and objectives by your actions. Confusion, fear, and uncertainty connected with low self-esteem can all be reduced and brought under relative control in this manner. Relative control is the key phrase here. The level of control that a person can achieve over his environment is directly related to his degree of organization. That must be kept constantly in mind, because without it the future is dismal—unless, of course, the woman you marry (keep the thought that she is no longer a girl) comes from a wealthy family. Doubtful at best, right? Therefore organize your priorities, methods, and goals as much as possible to give yourself a fighting chance. I'll demonstrate what I mean.

First, sit alone in a quiet place with no distractions or interruptions and list all the problems, worries, and difficulties that have become apparent in your life. The list usually is shorter than most people expect. Next, sort them into columns A, B, and C for "immediate attention," "future scheduling," and "whenever I get the time." Now concentrate on the A column and arrange the items in order of importance. The first four or five now represent your list of organizational priorities. As you'll remember, I mentioned four of my own, which are probably very similar to yours. They were limited income, lack of affordable housing, unfinished schooling, and lack of self-confidence. Take the items one by one and concentrate on them until you devise a feasible method to solve or at least lessen the urgency of each.

Let's begin with limited income. Raising a family is going to take money and lots of it. In my own case, my part-time salary of $4,264 a year wouldn't have been enough to keep us in dogfood and paper napkins, not to mention the hospital cost for having a baby ($6,300 in 1981).

At the time I was working as a salesperson/stockboy for a department store for slightly above minimum wage. When I naively asked my supervisor for a promotion because of my pressing situation, I was flatly turned down on the grounds of insufficient experience. I was, however, able to obtain a transfer to another department where a full-time employee was needed. The 25¢ per hour increase was no gold mine, but the extra fifteen hours and, more important, the accompanying health insurance benefits did make a difference. When the time came for the baby to be born, the hospital was one large bill that we no longer had to worry about.

Now that more money was coming into the household through my own efforts and my wife's part-time job as a restaurant cashier, the problem was how to keep expenses under control and channel the available funds only to necessities. The idea is to know where the money is being spent and redirect any wasted dollars to where they are most needed. That is where organization comes to the rescue, in the form of a budget.

Since we were still living with my parents, our first budget was rather lenient. It was to get much tighter and stricter after we were on our own and the baby was born, but it was helpful to get into the habit of budgeting our money early. The weekly draft looked something like this:

Combined Net Salary: $180
Gas: $25
Auto insurance: $18
Food: $20
Schooling costs: $20
Miscellaneous: $10

Great emphasis was on putting money into savings, which is where the remaining $87 would go. In the beginning it is best to have only a savings account rather than a checking account, for two main reasons. First, a savings account pays interest on your money, whereas most checking accounts offer only special banking privileges that you have no real need for yet. For example, paying bills by check instead of money order is merely a matter of convenience. Second, money tends to be spent faster through a checking account because of the ease of writing a check for virtually anything. Third, a person is less likely to spend money if he has to watch the cash leave his own hands. It takes time to appreciate and realize the connection between writing a check and spending money.

My next priority problem was finding affordable housing. When my wife and I were first married, she was not exactly enthused about living in such close quarters with my parents. Putting two housewives with their own ways of doing things under one roof is asking for trouble. Realistically, however, we had no other choice. We eventually reached a compromise under which I promised to have us moved out within two months if she would try to get along better with my parents in the meantime. Two months happened to fall precisely on Christmas; however, it was not until nearly Easter that we were able to make our move, and then only by a rather morbid stroke of luck.

My uncle had passed away a few months before our wedding, and my aunt continued on her own. However, the memories, the work, and the upkeep of their small duplex proved to be too much for her to handle alone. She offered to sell the house to my parents below current market value and at a lower rate of interest. The investment was a good one. Although the down payment was difficult for my parents, between our modest rent and the rent from tenants in the rear apartment, the monthly mortgage payment was virtually covered. The assistance was generous and timely, since our baby son arrived just two weeks before we were able to move into our new apartment.

My son was born April 1, 1982—April Fool's Day. I had promised my wife before she entered the hospital that I would stay with her throughout her labor and delivery of the baby. That was, of course, while we still thought it would be a natural childbirth. However, after nearly twelve futile hours of labor, the doctors decided on a Caesarean section as being in the best interests of both mother and child.

My wife wasn't too thrilled about the idea of surgery, but after so many hours of labor pains she would have agreed to nearly anything. However, she wanted me to keep my promise and stay with her in the operating room. I expected (or hoped) that the doctors would refuse permission, but to my reluctant surprise they encouraged my presence. Well, you only live once, right? So you might as well see how the whole thing starts.

She was awake and alert during the entire operation, since they had used a local anaesthetic that affected only the lower part of her body. A sheet was hung vertically in front of her face as she lay on her back so that she could not see what they were doing, but I unfortunately could. As the doctors made the incision, I held her hand and talked with her. She kept asking me to look over the sheet and tell her if they were almost finished. As a result, I am one man who can honestly say he knows his wife inside and out. The only time I started to feel sick was when the doctors tugged to remove the baby. Happily, it was only a few moments before the doctor handed my new son to the nurse, who handed him to me. She snapped a photo of the newborn boy, the proud father, and the exhausted mother at that unique time and setting before taking them to different sections of the hospital for specialized care.

Besides witnessing the miracle of human birth, I formed an opinion from the experience that will last forever. After watching so many hours of my wife's suffering and pain, I sincerely thank God that men can't have babies.

When we took our son home to his own room in our new apartment, I hoped it was the beginning of a more calm and settled period that lay ahead. I was now married, my job was paying better, we were in our own home, and the baby had been born all in just seven short months. What else could happen?

Usually when that particular question is asked, something is seriously wrong. My trouble was signaled by a layoff slip accompanying my paycheck at work. I had lost my job. Business was slow and profits were down, so there was no need to keep full-time employees on the payroll. The unemployment insurance check based on my slim wages gave me an early hint of what social security would probably be like. It was wholly inadequate to provide for even our basic needs. Every cent we had managed to save during the past months while living at my parents' home thus became our most important "security blanket."

Once again I say the magic word: organization. Think of it as a trustworthy and helpful friend to whom you can turn in time of need. This friend, however, does have certain limitations. A method's effectiveness is only as good as its planning. It's always comforting to formulate a plan of action beforehand to spare yourself the frustration and anger caused by relying on fickle chance. It takes time and effort to do the research and thought involved in the planning process of organization, but it saves countless hours of work and stress in the long run. It is true that there are no shortcuts in life, but the road can be made easier if one is willing to stop and take the time to think ahead.

For us, thinking ahead meant that we had enough money saved to cover our bills and expenses for about a month after my layoff date. I had to find a job within the first two weeks to meet this deadline, since most companies follow the procedure of witholding an employee's first week's paycheck. In those two weeks I developed and implemented what can best be described as an organized assault on the local job market.

A good opening move in job-hunting is to inform the people around you at home, at your former place of employment, and at school of the situation and ask them to let you know of any opportunities that may arise. The more eyes that are helping you to look, the more you may see. For your own benefit, keep open as many lines of communication as possible.

Second, answer specific want ads that appear to be the most promising. The best positions are filled quickly, so it's best to call and verify the current status of the ad. Has the job been filled or is it still available for interview?

Third, alphabetically follow one of the most concise and complete listings of employers that are available to a dedicated job-hunter: the telephone book's Yellow Pages. Visiting and filling out applications at an average of five stores a day enabled me to cover nearly fifty businesses in those two weeks.

Never leave a résumé unless you are specifically requested to do so. The ultimate goal of an application is to obtain an interview that may lead to a position. If too much information is given beforehand, there may be no need for an interview and therefore no job.

The purpose of the interview itself is to allow the employer to judge your character and potential through various personal and professional questions and decide whether or not you are the right person for the job. Be well prepared and articulate in your answers by knowing as much as possible both about your former job and the company for which you are presently interviewing. Also, never "bad-mouth" or insult your former employer in any way. It shows lack of courtesy and professional conduct.

Using this three-part method, I was able to obtain four employment offers worth considering without having to change my occupation and start from the beginning once again. Of the four, I chose one that was suggested to me by a former co-worker. She knew an assistant manager in a competing chain of stores and recommended me for employment. The assistant manager, having no openings in his store, brought me to the attention of his supervisors, who contacted me through their personnel department. I was given an interview and was offered the position of department manager in a store thirty-eight miles away in the next county. The money was better, and it meant promotion from salesman to manager, so in spite of the commuting distance involved, I accepted the job with the understanding that I would be transferred to a closer store in the near future. That understanding was eventually to cause problems resulting in my resignation, but for the moment I had solved the immediate need of a source of income.

Since my wife had stopped working just before our son was born, my income was now all we had. People had advised me to put the baby into the care of a sitter or day-care center, but even then—before the recent atrocities were made public—I didn't trust anyone with our child except close relatives. A child should grow with his parents even if they themselves aren't yet fully grown. I could deal with the loss of income but not with the constant worry that our son might be left unwatched, neglected, or far worse.

Our household budget had to be adapted to suit the financially tight situation. Again, only necessities were considered.

Net Weekly Salary: $140
Gas: $25
Auto insurance: $13
Food and baby: $25
Electric: $12
Phone: $7
Rent: $50   TOTAL: $132

We had a grand total of $8 a week left over to cover any nonbudgeted expenses. Those often included auto and home repairs, baby clothes, dental care, and many other unexpected but certainly necessary costs. In emergencies, we sometimes borrowed from one budget category to cover such expenses and paid it back the following week. This "borrowing from Peter to pay Paul" is a bad but sometimes useful habit.

Schooling was a category included in the family budget before we left my parents' home. However, there was no longer enough money to pay for my enrollment in community college. I was now in the middle of my second year as a Political Science/Public Administration student, and I certainly did not want to quit. Working with people on a daily basis as I had done in retailing, I was very much aware of the importance of an education to one's future. Intelligence, personality, and experience often mean nothing to a company in terms of promotability when they are not supported by a diploma (high school or college). I desperately did not want to be limited to the same type of work at forty as I was at nineteen. Sociologists call that social stratification. Without a diploma it takes extraordinary luck to break out of its barriers. And who wants to base an entire future on luck? Certainly not someone who's going to be successful. Success takes only a minimal amount of what is known as luck or good fortune, the other ingredients being ambition, hard work, and dedication. Those last three qualities are what it takes to earn a diploma, which is why it is so important in the job market for getting ahead in any career. It is also why, for the future of myself and my family, I didn't want to give it up.

Unfortunately, earning a college diploma calls for one more realistic ingredient: money. As I said, that was something that was in short supply. I brooded over the situation for several days before coming to the realization that if I had no money for college, someone must have it to lend. That someone was the federal government. What especially surprised me was the fact that I didn't have to rob Fort Knox to get the amount I needed. I had been misled to believe that you had to be practically poverty-stricken and a disabled minority-group member to obtain financial aid of any kind. That may be exaggerating a bit, but it was the prevailing belief among students at the time. Judging by what I have recently been told by students, the feeling has not changed much in recent years. Various financial aids, student grants, and scholarships are in fact available but are widely unused by qualified recipients.

Of the colleges that I queried to verify this trend, the available funds being used ranged from a mere 26 per-

cent to 73 percent. Colleges that need student enrollment to justify the costs of expansion programs do not
want to return loan funds to the federal government;
they want to use them to attract more people to their
campus.

The current belief among students that there is no
loan money or that the qualifications are too selective
and restrictive is, I suspect, largely caused by two types
of people: those who have never applied for a grant
and those who have been rejected because their family
income is such that they can easily afford the costs. I
myself was able to obtain only about half of my tuition
through financial aid for the latter reason. The remaining
half came from my parents, who were once again willing
to shoulder additional expense in the cause of my future.
I was therefore able to continue my education.

Finally, after all that has been said in this chapter, we
can address the matter of self-confidence. However, it is
a priority that by now should require no discussion.
Every occurring problem that is successfully solved, no
matter how large or how small, adds to your credit as an
independent and capable father. Merely having to ask
for help along the way does not make you indecisive or
weak. It shows inner strength and wisdom in being able
to obtain what is necessary to achieve your defined goals.
Asking for help becomes dependency only when a
person is no longer willing to try to do without it. The
fact that problems are being solved by your own efforts
and planning, with so many trials both behind and in
front of you as a struggling teenage father, should
convince anyone that you are a winner. People may not
envy your position, but they will respect your character;
and, after all, your position will eventually change but

your character will not. Organize, sacrifice, and do what is necessary to survive and succeed, and the self-confidence of a winner will not be something you have to show: It will be something you cannot hide.

Quirks and Quarrels

Now that you have dealt with some of the chal-
lenges of the outside world, you must confront
those of your inside environment as well, name-
ly the family. Foremost in this very special little place
is your wife. If you have not had the experience of living
with a sister close to your own age, you're in for a demonstration of human behavior that will stagger your imagination. In some ways, women are more confusing
and unpredictable than interest rates, and even more
difficult to understand.

Everything from poetry to psychological analysis has
been written in the attempt to explain women. The
trouble is that most of it has been written by men. What
man can truthfully understand the logic of hanging
pantyhose over a shower curtain, owning sixteen pairs of
shoes when there are only seven days in a week, and
wearing four-inch heels that would reduce even the most
hardened Russian ballerina to tears? Then there's the
matter of diets. One week it's lettuce and carrots, and
the next it's fudge sundaes and chocolate bars. What
makes sense? Of course our brief discussion of female

habits would not be complete without mentioning the downright peculiar practice of keeping a four-month supply of disposable tampons in the closet in case of an unexpected flood or nuclear war.

In the interests of fairness and objectivity, I must also comment on the legitimate gripes that women in general have against their husbands. They must have a hard time understanding why we have a side escape in our jockey shorts that we never bother to use; how we can misplace everything from a power drill to sneakers in the space of a half hour; and how we can complain about the house being a mess when we have thrown our jacket over a chair, spread the newspaper on the sofa, put our briefcase, tie, and money on the television set, and left our shoes in the center of the room. And there's more. Men have the set opinion that women don't work. If that is so, then fixing breakfast, making beds, dressing kids, washing laundry, ironing clothes, scrubbing floors, vacuuming carpets, dusting furniture, grocery shopping, making dinner, and washing dishes must all be truly enjoyable. Who could ever wish for more? Maybe that could explain their behavior.

The purpose of this sarcastic tirade is to demonstrate the fact that when passionate and lustful love has been replaced by more realistic marital love, a person's view of the partner tends to change. The transition is commonly known as "the honeymoon's over" syndrome. The husband may find that his wife's golden blonde hair that had first attracted him comes from a bottle, or a wife may discover that her husband has the habit of wearing the same T-shirt for four days straight. In such cases, disillusionment can easily cause conflict.

Occasional quarrels are a natural and healthy part of

any relationship; they can serve to settle differences before they become major problems. But too much of anything can be harmful, and if quarreling is incessant the marriage may be in serious trouble.

Specifically, arguments are outward verbal or physical demonstrations of destructive and aggressive behavior. They are most frequently the response to the anger and hostility caused by personal frustration. All frustration sooner or later results in some direct or disguised form of aggression. The aggression may be aimed at perceived or convenient sources of that frustration, which, unfortunately, are usually those people who are closest to us such as a wife or a child. It may also be displaced on an object such as a dish smashed or a door kicked.

A most effective approach in dealing with this destructive energy is early detection and recognition of its harmful effects. That is not always easy to do, since the symptoms may be directed inward by a person who, for various reasons, is trying to deal with his or her problems alone. That is not what marriage is about.

My own personal pastime for a long time was pouting. It can't be stated any other way. All I gained from those hours of sitting alone feeling sorry for myself because of the frustrations of being a teenage father was the attainment of the perfect pout. Nothing was resolved or gained until I learned to open up and talk with my wife and give her the consideration that I felt the world was denying me. Unless home can be made into a place free of mistrust, inhibition, and tension, where personal problems can be discussed and resolved between *two adults*, life is going to be no laughing matter.

CHAPTER 4

Insults and Answers

L earning to answer insults and criticism is often the most difficult and unpleasant task a teenage father must face when starting a family of his own. By understanding the nature and origin of the insensitivity present in the world today, one can better learn to handle offensive remarks and implications when faced with them in everyday life.

Dealing with insults, criticism, and abusive comments from those around us has been a part of our lives since childhood. We may look back a few years at the epithets "Tinsel Teeth," "Birdlegs," or "Hippo Hips" and remember the bitterness they caused or laugh at their utter insignificance. Children and adolescents can be particularly cruel in applying such nicknames, but by the same token they can be especially hurt, since they frequently judge themselves and their achievements in the light of others' opinions. Constant disparaging comments can lead to abandonment of ambition and reinforcement of a self-image that says, "I can't do anything right" or "I'm a nobody."

The same may still be true of us young adults. A boss

or supervisor may still call us an idiot or useless because, perhaps, we failed to do something on time or did it too slowly to satisfy his or her personal pace. The justification for such abuse, whether from a precocious five-year-old or an eighty-two-year-old woman, is invariably that it was necessary in an effort to correct some perceived fault or flaw, which may or may not be real. Rarely, however, is criticism balanced with enough understanding and encouragement to offset the negative effects of unrelenting and often unwarranted scrutiny.

People may also feel a need to demonstrate their superiority to convince themselves, as well as others, of the power and prestige of their own position. Language is a good gauge of a person's true outlook. Listen to the difference in meanings between the statements, "I am the best at what I am doing," and "I am doing the best I can." One is simply a pompous boast designed to elicit awe from an admiring audience, whereas the other can be considered a reasonable self-evaluation.

Anyone who has ever worked in a service-oriented occupation (jobs dealing directly with the public) can testify to this seemingly innate need in the vast majority of people to assert their superiority without regard to others' feelings. However, don't misunderstand my point. Controlling the course of your own life is essential for success, but manipulating the lives of others by attempting to bring them around to our way of thinking is a risky game. Unfortunately, it is also a game nearly everyone likes to play. Magnified to the level of nations, it becomes a chief source of war.

Between two people, the game is most easily played by the use of derogatory comments or insults. Calling someone stupid for having made an error somehow makes us feel superior—even if we made the same mistake ourselves the week before. Tomorrow we may make a similar mistake and hope that no one like ourselves will catch us at it.

Also to be considered is the fact that chronological age does not assure maturity in accepting other people's faults. We must learn to treat others as we wish to be treated. "Do unto others as you would have others do unto you." The logic of this biblical admonition is accepted by every civilized religion. The more the pity that after so many centuries it's still often ignored, proving the point that as people grow older they do not necessarily become wiser. They may merely become more experienced and skillful at handling the criticisms and insults that they have faced all their lives.

As children, the great pain we inflicted on our peers with cruel remarks equaled the pain we ourselves felt when we were similarly attacked. With time and age, we learn to accept our own faults and become less sensitive to the comments of others. Rarely, however, do we mature enough to gain the wisdom and understanding to make the Golden Rule a part of our philosophy. Why? Besides being unnatural in today's world of business, whose "rules" include "Go for the throat" and "Kick 'em when they're down," it is not yet practical. Business means competition, and, as we shall see later, competition means more than simply winning or losing. It means comparing yourself to others as a measure of your own abilities. Since most people fall short of their own expectations, to gain an advantage they are more likely to "do unto others" first.

The job that you accept or continue to work at to support your new family may very well be the first in your life that you must hold to survive. One thing must be clearly understood: Paying for food and rent is much different than working to get a car stereo-tapedeck or a new album. If such items are features of your first family budget, I would strongly suggest that you reconsider your priorities. As you will soon learn, working because you want to work and working because you have to work are totally different propositions. In either case, however, if keeping your job matters, then satisfying your boss matters even more.

If your boss tends to be somewhat temperamental, try to keep in mind that persons in authority are a different species altogether when it comes to making mistakes. Their specific job is to correct fault wherever it may occur, but when the fault lies in themselves they are placed in a particularly awkward situation. That applies especially to middle-level supervisors, who must appear infallible and all-knowing to those under their direction and at the same time subservient, loyal, and trustworthy to their own supervisors, who in some cases answer only to the corporate president and God.

Everyone must eventually answer to some boss or high command, even if it is his wife. I've seen managers who could growl like a wounded bear for eight hours straight suddenly turn into Winnie-the-Pooh when their wife walked into the store.

Perhaps this dual role combined with job pressures is the reason for the supervisory temperament. After all, the drop to the bottom is much farther when you're at the top. The old adage, "The bigger they are, the harder they fall," is still true. Understanding that may make it easier for you to tolerate a supervisor's unreasonable demands or criticism and hold on to a much needed job.

The human propensity for momentary stupidity or absentmindedness happily does not play favorites according to position. We've all done things that we're not particularly proud of, but few will get skewered from so many directions as those unfortunate people who must satisfy both upper and lower demands. At the entry level of any career, those are the people you must learn to deal with and accept as part of a changing environment as you move past them in your own journey to success.

Nothing is so constant as change. Our society is extremely mobile; people change jobs or job locations as frequently as the seasons change. Out of curiosity, I figured out the average length of time that a given supervisor remained my boss over the course of my five jobs. A mere 192 days! I could last that long in the army! So whether your immediate supervisor is a teacher, a sales manager, or a head mechanic, chances are that he or she is merely a temporary figure with whom you must contend.

As with all people, the personalities of supervisors range from fair and understanding to impossible. If you have a severe or continuing problem with the person in charge, don't simply quit. Besides the damage that will do to your bank account, it is evidence of immaturity and irrational behavior—and will not get you a good job reference.

A good rule to remember is to respect the position if not the person. Of course, it never hurts to hunt for a better job on the side, but there will always be a boss to deal with, no matter what job you take. That's why so many people go into business for themselves: to be their own boss. However, that alternative is usually impossible for a beginner in the world of work; it requires both experience and capital.

Adaptability in dealing with people in authority is something we must all learn quickly. The spoiled youngster must learn to get along with other children and respect the position of the teacher or face negative reactions and harsh consequences. The word "respect" should be noted here, since we, as children, learn to obey and follow the lead of those people who possess qualities that we admire, such as intelligence, kindness, wisdom, or power.

The periodic conduct report sent to the child's home with the report card is intended to elicit the cooperation and support of the parents while instilling in the child an attitude that is more receptive to society's demands. Our behavior and personality are thus early conditioned in such a way that we instinctively react and often conform to the expectations and criticisms of three distinct social groups: parents and close relatives, the public and everyday acquaintances, and our own persuasive force. Obviously, not all are authority figures, but through our developed respect for them each offers input that we incorporate into an internal set of accepted values (conscience) and standards as to how a respected person in authority should act. For example, we don't see too many prominent people belching in public; therefore, most of us would not consider doing it ourselves.

A failure to conform to these relative social standards, combined with the inherent human need to evidence supremacy, is ultimately the source of all criticism and insult. More simply stated, the closer our behavior matches either the flattering or dismal expectations of others, the less fault-finding and correction we must endure.

Children, being naturally open and honest with their feelings, combine both of these motives for behavior when applying epithets to others. They thus loudly proclaim what is and is not acceptable to society as it has been shown to them by the three important groups. Let's look at each of those groups separately and see how their influence continues to affect us through the years.

The first and most enduring model on which we base appropriate behavioral patterns is our relationship with our parents and, to a lesser extent, close family members. From the moment we are taken as a newborn from the hospital, wrapped in a blue blanket for a boy or a pink one for a girl, social conditioning has begun. Through our respect and love for our parents, they become our first and most highly regarded critics. This deep feeling does dissipate during the years of teenage rebellion, no matter how it appears to parents at the time. Instead, it is overshadowed by an obsessively strong preoccupation with understanding the many pressures and changes that are occurring at that age. By re-evaluating and measuring what we have been told for nearly fifteen years is correct against what we now perceive as true, we are transformed from dependent teenager to independent adult.

This natural process of growth cannot be derailed. Our appreciation and love for our parents returns fourfold in our early twenties, when we realize that their protective guidance and resulting criticism were no harsher during the unsettling teenage period than they had been when we were children. Nor were they intended as a direct attack against us as persons, although being independent does involve accepting criticism. The parental criticism had not actually changed at all through the years—we changed.

Recently there was a story in the newspapers about a man who was celebrating his hundredth birthday. To give you an idea of how long ago that was, in 1884 Grover Cleveland was President, there were only thirty-seven states in the Union, and the Statue of Liberty was still two years from completion. A reporter asked, "What is the fondest memory of your youth?" The man recalled a time when he was nine or ten years old living in southern Louisiana. Every Saturday morning his father would take him fishing at a nearby creek for an hour or two before going to work. The boy seldom had much luck during those outings, but one day he caught a large bass with his simple bamboo pole in the shallow waters. He vividly remembered his father's calling it the biggest fish he had ever seen caught in the creek and saying how proud he was of his son. "The fish couldn't have been that big, since it was a small creek," explained the old man, "but I smiled so much that my face hurt the next day." Remember that this had taken place nearly ninety years earlier, and still his father's approval was clear in his memory. Admittedly he sometimes could not recall what had happened the day before, but this small gesture of a parent's reinforcement had lasted a long lifetime.

As a teenage father, the support you receive from your own parents may be minimal until they eventually accept the situation as permanent. Their feelings of disappointment are difficult to ignore, but they can be overcome gradually by the confidence with which you handle the situation. Prove to them your mature abilities of control and thoughtful restraint. As was said at the beginning of this chapter, through understanding one can better learn to handle offensive remarks and inferences. The first, bitterest, and most critical remarks faced by a teenage father come, unfortunately, from those closest to him, those whose influence has been the greatest and whose opinions, if not always adopted, are respected the most.

Parents often view their children as extensions of themselves, and they unconsciously try to direct and steer them past the mistakes and missed opportunities of their own lives. After spending a decade and a half caring and planning ahead for you, the sudden drastic changes are emotionally confusing and result in frustration, hurt, and anger. The fact that you are no longer their little boy who needs an occasional bandage on a cut finger, a shoelace tied, or a reminder to wear a sweater on chilly mornings is an uncomfortable and often unnerving realization to parents. If they show bitterness, you must not let their momentary feelings become an ongoing part of your relationship with them. Bitterness breeds bitterness, just as hate reproduces in kind. Taking the time to understand their feelings and viewpoint is one way to lessen the pain inflicted by both sides during the first few months of adjustment when harsh criticism and ill will are likely to be abundant. Maintaining a firm policy of patient understanding has a much better chance of preventing any long-lasting effects than if one chooses simply to ignore the critical situation (if that were possible). Ignoring problems never leaves answers in its wake, just pain and cruel stupidity.

By becoming a husband and father while still in your teens, you have been prematurely thrown onto a course that is beyond the control of your parents or any close relatives.

The average American male marries first in his early to mid-twenties and does not have a child until considerably later. The three or four years between a person in his late teens and one in his early twenties is comparatively small when we consider current life expectancies of 69.9 years for a man and 77.8 years for a woman, but they are highly important in personal development. I am careful not to use the relative terms *man* and *boy* in this context because I'm sure some seventeen-year-olds could put to shame so-called men in their early twenties in regard to maturity. But that is the exception, not the rule. All of us develop at our own pace during those years, yet under difficult circumstances the natural rhythm of growth is quickened to enable us to learn what is necessary to survive. A street-wise fifteen-year-old in a rough neighborhood is a good example of this speeded development in the ability to adjust to a trying environment.

A teenage parent experiences something similar in trying to cope with the prospects of sudden adulthood. The insecure sense of "me against the world," which is common among teenagers, is heightened for a teenage parent. He must face the abrupt cutting off of parental ties and the familiar life-style of childhood and make the effort to stand independently as an adult. Cutting those ties and moving away from home to a new place with a new family means that he no longer has the behavioral model of an adult to observe directly. That model has, instead, become *you*, to pass on to your own children as a parent and a responsible member of society. As such, you are the role model of the future.

* * *

The second social group whose comments, opinions, and criticism shape our behavior is everyday acquaintances and the public at large. This category includes everyone in the world who is not related to us in any way. Heading the list is a boss or supervisor, discussed earlier. Just as our parents are the personal people whom we seemingly always try to impress and please, the boss is the most prominent member of the nonpersonal group to whom we try to demonstrate our abilities. The gap between the personal and nonpersonal relationships can never be completely crossed at the supervisor level. To do so would introduce personal feelings into the work situation that would affect even the most routine daily contacts and interfere with job efficiency. That is the principal reason that many companies and the government itself have rules against having even remote relatives working together. For example, a supervisor would not, and probably could not, judge an employee's work adequately if that employee were his own son.

I had an opportunity to witness an example of this rule of impersonality in business. In my second year of high school I made two friends—I'll call them Dave and John—who came to mean more to me than either of them will ever realize. We were nearly inseparable for the next three years and inevitably came to be called the Three Musketeers. We listened to one another's woes, drank, laughed, went to football games, movies, and arcades together, and defended each other in time of trouble. A threat to one was a threat to all. I'm glad I was able to experience that type of cameraderie at least once, but times change rapidly.

After graduation, John went to work as an electrician's apprentice while Dave and I attended a local college for a year and a half. After that Dave joined John as an apprentice. As the word apprentice implies, work in the skilled trades is based on a system of seniority. Even though both were classified as apprentices, John's senior position by reason of time on the job was understood, and the friendship, although markedly changed by circumstances, still endured. It was not until John was officially given the title foreman that open conflict replaced what had been cooperation and loyalty. Close friends, like relatives, cannot give each other orders or judge the other's work in the impersonal manner required in a work environment without its affecting the personal relationship. Two friends can work together, but one cannot supervise the other.

Soon sides were drawn as respective positions were established and defined. My attempt at nonpartisanship from the sidelines became impossible as I found myself favoring one side over the other. What had been three equal but separate parts became a coalition of two against one. Dave still works under and follows instructions from John, but he is now a boss, not a friend. As a result of our common stand against John, Dave and I became much closer through the years. Unfortunately, the special three-way friendship is gone, and unkind memories prevent its ever returning. That is the price of mixing "business" with pleasure.

Most business in the United States is service-oriented in nature. Chances are good that your first job will be in that sector, whether it's busing tables, running a cash register, or renting paddle boats to tourists. None of those occupations is particularly noteworthy in itself, but all deal with that fickle entity called the public.

People as a group are totally unpredictable. As a group they are worlds away from the first, more personal, social structure of the family, whose behavior patterns could more or less be depended upon to be consistent. Love and care are the binding emotions of the family, whereas money is the driving force behind the public as a whole. Sometimes mistakenly viewed as one and the same, these two different motives are in sharp contrast, as is evidenced by the different ways in which we interpret and accept or reject the criticisms of the two groups.

Parents' comments, like those of a close friend or relative, are based on their sometimes biased view and appraisal of you as a person, and therefore take on more personal meaning. We care about what they think of us. Paradoxically, their criticism demonstrates how much they care for us.

The critical comments of members of the public, on the other hand, are intended only to help them assert themselves over you. In pursuing their goal of material gain or convenience, they are totally unconcerned about you as a person.

In dealing with the public in my past jobs and my present one as a retail manager, I have served everyone from "bag ladies" to corporation executives. All must be treated equally, because in today's society no one can be quite sure if one of those ladies wasn't his boss.

No matter what job you take or aspire to, from rock star to hair stylist, one thing I can promise is that you will not find boredom in working with the public. Every moment and every situation is different. One person may shower you with compliments for a job well done while the next may castigate you for the very same work. Abuse comes with the territory when your job involves working with the public. Nevertheless, there are times when the impulse to lash out physically is difficult to suppress, and I'm forced to come up with a fast, effective, but nonoffensive response. One such remark came from a man in his forties with more rings on his fingers than Mr. T. Apparently they gave him a sense of self-importance. "Be a good boy and put this box into my cart," he said. My first impulse was a fast left hook, but out of nowhere came the answer: "I've got two boys of my own at home, so I don't think the term 'boy' really fits, do you?" "No," he said in obvious embarrassment, "it's okay. I'll do it myself."

The incident proved two things to me. First is the obvious: A person may make money, but money does not make a person. Second, the customer's backing down and doing the task himself, although actually it was part of my job, did show a rare acknowledgment of respect. The mere title "father," implied by my answer, in fact demands respect more than any display of jewelry could obtain. It is a social label that indicates maturity and the accepted responsibility of caring for a family. Remember that people learn early in life to recognize exceptional qualities in others. A man, not a boy, who places the needs of his family before his own and works to provide for them has certainly earned both the respect of a man from society and the love of his family as a father.

Understandably, these values are difficult to remember in the workplace when someone, customer or otherwise, is insulting you. Bad as that can be, however, I've always found much worse the sotto voce remarks that aren't meant to be heard. They are especially infuriating because the person hasn't the courage or decency to confront you openly and give you a chance to defend yourself. This is often the case in upper levels of management when supervisors are defending their jobs and reputations (as you must do) against those who wish to see them replaced.

Interestingly, most bosses won't let their employees take verbal abuse from anyone but themselves. That kind of selfishness can be oddly reassuring as to support: If your boss is satisfied, criticism from anyone else shouldn't really matter.

The support of a trusted co-worker can also be comforting in difficult circumstances. Whether the offensive remarks or actions come from customers or other co-workers, you can be sure your friend has been through similar situations at one time or another and is standing beside you. His or her calm advice may help you avoid an angry response that you might later regret.

Having examined the social categories of parents and of the public, let us move on to the third and perhaps most ignored influence in our lives: the power of ourselves. First, however, let us look at a different aspect of criticism.

Like everything natural in life, the tendency of human beings to criticize their surroundings has both good and bad features. After all, there is no day without night, no fast without slow, no right without left. . .well, you get the idea. Therefore, despite all the negative effects of criticism, it must also bring some good. This positive aspect is known as constructive criticism. It is evidenced in such cases as talking a drunken friend out of driving home, helping someone to stop smoking, protesting a law that is unfair, or teaching a child right from wrong. The art of teaching, itself, is the most practical and common application of this concept of constructive criticism. Teachers everywhere instruct their students, no matter how young or how old, through a combination of encouragement and correction. As a father who will before long be teaching your child and answering his or her questions, this is an important point. Encouraging someone to improve himself and act in a desired way with praise instead of condemnation is constructive. Showing him how to do so by correcting errors and observed faults is healthy criticism.

This healthy and productive criticism, which we can apply to all objects and areas of society, is what is guaranteed to us in the Bill of Rights. We have a culture with a conscience. Our freedom of speech and right to criticize are what we cherish so dearly as a nation and a people. They set us apart from most other countries of the world. No government anywhere, however, can restrict how much we influence one particular member of society with our opinions. Our demands and expectations of him are often unreasonably high and bring upon him exceptionally cruel criticism for failure. You may have guessed that the unfortunate individual referred to is ourselves. It is true that we are often our own worst critic. For that reason, we must include ourselves when we discuss critics who most influence us during the course of our life. No one will ever judge us as harshly—perhaps as accurately—as we judge ourselves.

This self-evaluation, which one could almost call

sadistic, may be intensified by still another factor. Some-times assuming the terms of a challenge, contention, struggle, or rivalry, the forms and effects of the factor called competition are widespread and unmistakable.

As a teenage father, you have much tough and trying competition ahead of you. The ability of a father, at no matter what age, to provide for his family is based on his use of superior qualities and talents for survival. That skill is acquired by the experience gained in dealing with others over a considerable period of time, which many young fathers lack. However, that disadvantage may be overcome or at least minimized by understanding the basic concepts of competition and applying them with strong determination and motivation.

It has been said that Americans love competition and that they do not tolerate losers. I agree with only one of those statements. Americans certainly like to compete by established rules. We recognize the benefits of open competition, and we base our entire economic system of free enterprise on its proven values. The absence of free enterprise under communism is why we are repelled by that system as a way of life. But no matter how much control is imposed on a society, complete restriction is impossible. Competition is a natural instinct common to all human beings. It is necessary for survival and is clearly seen in the animal kingdom, where the outcome means life or death. Deriving pleasure or amusement from competition, however, is strictly a human trait.

In any competition, whether the stakes are simple satisfaction or the cost of a life, both a winner and a loser are essential. The degree of tolerance and consideration granted to the loser is what separates humans from animals in nature, and democracies from dictatorships among nations. America stands out as a shining example of that tolerance. Free competition, without fear of persecution for failure, is the magnet that has always attracted people from other lands. In short, tolerance for losers is what has made America a winner.

Learn a lesson from that fact in your dealings with others. A defeated competitor harshly treated will always be looking for an opportunity to even the score and will eventually succeed in doing so, at your expense. However, if you can win respect as both a good winner and a good loser, you will have acquired a valuable asset that you can call upon in future dealings with others.

By looking at competition on a personal level, we can see why it is a major cause of self-criticism. Competition involves both meeting what we believe to be the expectations of others and showing our superiority by surpassing those expectations. In "keeping up with the Joneses," we compare ourselves to others while forgetting the special qualities that each of us has that others don't possess. Undue self-criticism arises solely from failing to realize our positive assets in competition. While striving to be stronger, smarter, faster, cleverer, and more daring, we lose ourselves in the process. If we can't reach our own potential, we certainly can't hope to match anyone else's. We must not sacrifice our strengths in compensating for our weaknesses.

As we have seen, our society is based on a naturally competitive system. Just as we must learn to respect other people, we must learn to compete and deal with others to achieve our needs and desires. We must appreciate the reality that people like competition because it gives them the opportunity to demonstrate their abilities in the areas in which they excel. When faced with any contest or challenge, you can give yourself the best chance of success by using the method athletes call "psyching yourself up"; that is, concentrating on your own positives and emphasizing them over your more vulnerable features.

When we criticize ourselves for every shortcoming or minor failure, we are maximizing our faults and thus helping to strengthen our opponent's position. To succeed, simply practice being good at what you are good at and, most important, believe in yourself. Make your rivals and opponents play *your* game on *your* terms, and the odds will swing greatly in your favor. You know better than anyone else what you are capable of accomplishing, and you should stress those positive qualities. Thus, the struggle is more within ourselves than against others as we attempt to satisfy our own expectations of ourselves. That is a competitive test that is much more difficult than matching the expectations of others. As in all competitions, we are the ultimate judge of ourselves. The only criticisms that matter are the ones that we choose to accept. In the competition between our own self-image and the image relayed to us through other people's comments, victory can best be described as mind over insult. You are what you think you are; it's as simple as that.

As a young man who has recently become both a father and a husband, you may be a bit confused as to what each role involves. You may not even be totally clear as to who you are. What you must remember is that you must love and care for someone else more than you would for yourself. Your reward will be the comfort of a close-knit family whose support and understanding will shield you against any outside criticism.

When that family itself is verbally attacked, however, we usually respond by trying to ram that shield down the offender's throat, no matter what the odds. Children unconsciously realize that fact and use it to provoke an immediate reaction from peers who are physically weaker than themselves. By so doing, they select easy prey who are drawn into a nearly hopeless contest; their sole aim is humiliating their victim. Remember that the display of supremacy is a basic reason for insults.

Adults do the same thing, although perhaps not so bluntly, having learned through the years to conceal their methods. However, the basic motive remains: to achieve a hasty reaction without allowing you to think and turn it to your own advantage. Competition for a prized job or social standing is often characterized by such behavior. Remember, compete only when you are prepared. Don't act on someone else's cue, because that cue comes only when the opponent is well prepared for you.

The world will always be full of competitive and critical people trying to arrange their surroundings to suit their needs instead of adjusting their needs to meet their surroundings. In so doing, they must compete for what is yours as you compete for what is theirs. As a young father, you have a fierce drive motivated by love, devotion, and sacrifice that other people don't understand. It frightens them. People don't like what they can't understand, and therefore they criticize it and you. Not only have you been able to adapt your needs to conquer a difficult situation with determination and skill, which many don't have, but you have also set yourself apart by the speed with which you were able to make the transition from son to father and, in many cases, from boy to man. You are undeniably special, and special people often are forced to face ridicule. Being able to face it only adds to your prestige, which others try to destroy.

Learning to recognize insults and their sources and to understand and handle them while turning them to your own advantage is a recognized skill in itself; in large part it is the stuff of public relations. The way you view yourself through comments, either constructive or abusive, could be the difference between success and failure. It must be treated seriously; if it is not, the damage to your potential may be irreparable. It has been said that the saddest damage that can occur is that which could have been prevented. Learning to tune out insults (mere words) while tuning in real threats to your family (education, health, job security, good housing) is the best preventive plan of action. It is, in fact, the only practical answer to insults.

CHAPTER ◇ 5

Baby Makes Three

C hapter 1 was based on fact, Chapter 2 on procedure, Chapter 3 on comedy, and Chapter 4 on
serious understanding. In a way, this chapter
combines all four characteristics: It is about love. Not the
type of love embodied in the lyrics of a popular song, but
the unique feeling engendered by the presence of one's
own newborn baby.

The word love is often taken for granted as its definition becomes more vaguely interpreted. For a school
assignment on the meaning of the word, I was in fact
able to collect no less than twenty-eight definitions, and
a classmate managed to find nearly sixty in her research.
Sixty different ways to describe love, and still no one
knows exactly what it is!

The same is true for hatred, sadness, jealousy, and
many other emotions, since they are feelings that can
only be described, not defined.

Of all the emotions, love is by far the strongest, and in
particular parental love for a child cannot be equaled.
There is something about the tininess, helplessness, and
dependency of a baby that is capable of drawing inner

feelings of warmth and caring from even the coldest of people. Manufacturers design hundreds of kinds of infant dolls, from Cabbage Patch Kids to Muppet Babies, to capitalize on the parental instinct that exists even in very young children.

To romanticize the birth of a child to two people, one might call it the result of their unity in love. It is a permanent tie that can never be destroyed. Cynics may say that the woman or man simply forgot to take precautions, and it's true that becoming a father before the age of twenty usually involves the latter. In either case, however, the birth of a child has certain "magical" effects on both the couple and their surroundings.

Despite the difficult circumstances at the time, I was proud as punch when my first son was born. Like most men, I had hoped for a boy to follow in my footsteps and carry on the family name, not to mention all the fun I was going to have playing games with him as he grew up.

Confident but not quite certain beforehand that it would be a boy, I nonetheless bought a room full of typical "boy stuff" such as football, baseball and plastic bat, wind-up toy train, guitar, and Fisher Price toys galore. All were prepared for his arrival even before I had a place for him to sleep. Baby furniture, even used, is more expensive than I had realized. However, friends and just plain luck came to my rescue; people do care about other people, especially when a child is concerned.

A fellow worker who heard that my wife was soon to have a baby generously offered to give us her crib, since she had firmly decided to have no more children. I'm not sure whether her husband had had a say in that decision. Other items such as high chair and carriage were obtained through the help of relatives. We learned that garage and yard sales were excellent, fairly inexpensive sources of needed furniture and other items. At that point inexpensive was the operative word in our planning.

The real drawback to the situation was that with each new object we obtained, our 11' × 14' room in my parents' house became increasingly cramped. Soon the narrow aisle beside the bed disappeared as things accumulated and stacked along the walls for the past months slowly crept toward the center of the room. It simply wasn't meant to hold three dressers, two desks, one large bookcase and a crib, along with the queen-size bed and assorted other pieces packed away in an endless number of cardboard boxes. The "cave," as the room became known, was filled to capacity and beyond as we tried to fit everything we owned into its limited area. Everything but my car, of course, which itself had been turned into a storage room. We didn't realize at the time, however, that crowded as the room may have been, we were lucky to have a roof over our heads, thanks to the care and patience of my parents.

Two weeks before we were scheduled to move into our new apartment, our son, Michael, was born. After watching the ordeal of the Caesarean operation, my nerves were shot. I was quite composed during the surgery itself, but afterwards I couldn't hold a cup of coffee steady as I slowly came to realize what I had actually seen.

That inconvenience couldn't stop me and my paternal pride from gathering the snapshots that the nurses had taken and showing them off at work and half a dozen other places—much to the later disapproval of my wife.

In a calmer frame of mind, I returned to the hospital that night with a friend to visit the nursery and view my new son. Many people were waiting to see sons, daughters, brothers, sisters, nieces, and nephews of their own. One thing about the group remains in my memory, however. I had been told that women get a certain look in their eyes when they see a newborn baby, a kind of all-encompassing look whose meaning is unmistakable. The urge to be a mother is evidently strong, as the frequent glances and outright stares we received seemed to prove. My friend had the same feeling, although I never mentioned a word of it to him, and I said, "I'm ineligible for such looks now; I've done my part, now it's your turn." Jokingly, he replied, "We should have known about this place years ago. Just think of all the gas we could have saved cruising in a car."

Finally a nurse raised the shade over the window near my son's plastic, see-through crib, and I got down to the business of closely "evaluating" my son for the first time.

"He's got my wife's face except for the eyes; those are mine," I observed. As he started to cry along with the other babies, my friend smartly remarked, "Yeah, and he's got your mouth too!" Watching the tiny premature babies with tubes and wires attached to them in a special section toward the back of the nursery, I was simply glad that my boy was healthy, no matter what he looked like.

We only had to spend a week in the "cave" with our new son before it was time to move into the apartment, which by comparison was a palace. Although we had established one of the two bedrooms as Michael's room, we kept him in a bassinet in our room for the first three weeks. He was so tiny and fragile that we wanted to watch him carefully.

He was so tiny and fragile, but the first thing you really discover about babies once you get them home is how demanding they can be. They don't care if you're sick or exhausted; they want what they want, and they want it now! The nighttime feedings can be especially trying for new parents. I was good about helping my wife for a while. After that I elbowed her out of bed when he cried at 2 a.m.—and sometimes even when I only thought I heard him cry. My excuse (which works to this day with my second son) is that I need all my strength for work the next day. She is supposed to draw her energy for days on end from two hours of sleep at night, hot coffee, cold showers, and an hour-long "catnap" in the afternoon. To my continued amazement, she is able to do just that—even now, with two kids.

At about three months Michael developed the first signs of colic. He became increasingly restless, staying awake all night long and almost all day. His violent outbursts of cries and high-pitched screams made it obvious that he was in severe pain. When we tried to comfort him he stiffened his entire body as firm as a board in a frightening position. Happily, because of early diagnosis and treatment, he had a relatively short bout with the sickness, but the experience did nothing to improve my negative childhood opinion of doctors.

As events turned out, it was only appropriate that the doctor who attended Michael in the hospital be the one to solve the problem of his illness, since he was the person responsible for the mistake that caused it. In the hospital, a certain feeding formula is prescribed that the doctor believes best suits the needs of that particular infant. Shortly before Michael developed colic, his formula had been switched to a brand that contains iron. The change, we correctly suspected, had something to do with what suddenly went wrong with our child. His

stomach apparently could not digest the additional nu-
trients, which caused the severe cramps and spasms associated with the disorder. Michael improved rapidly
after being returned to his original formula. Soon he was
his old fussy, demanding self again, and we wouldn't
have had it any other way.

Despite the small crises that arise and the routine that
parents must become accustomed to during the early
months of parenthood, the development of a child during that period is amazing to watch. It goes so fast that
one must be keenly alert even to notice changes.

All infants vary greatly in their physical and mental
growth and awareness of their surroundings according to
a biological process called maturation. All living things
develop consistently according to an inborn genetic code
or plan. In some species the plan is preset and precise,
allowing for little physical or behavioral variety within
the species. A potted fern is a potted fern, just as a mosquito is a mosquito. See one and basically you've seen
them all. In human beings, however, the plan is flexible
and allows for some physical and a great many behavioral
differences. No two people, not even identical twins, are
exactly alike. From the moment of birth, newborns show
differences in behavior and temperament.

Maturation itself is a series of preprogrammed
changes that occur not only in the form of an organism,
but also in its intelligence, complexity, and functioning.
It is the unfolding of inherited potential through genetics.
We can become only what we are capable of becoming.
Faulty nutrition, neglect, or illness can delay the process
of maturation at any age, but it is particularly harmful to
young children, who are developing both physically and
mentally at a faster rate than at any other time in their

life. The quality of a child's diet, especially under the age of two, is crucial to his development. Anything that impedes his progress at this stage may cause brain damage and other severe injuries that are permanent— and for a child that is a very long time.

On the other hand, proper nutrition, a healthful environment, and even encouragement and teaching will not speed up a child's development dramatically, but they will enable the child to reach his or her potential; then the only obstacle to success becomes himself and his natural limitations.

To remove all other obstacles is the responsibility of the parents, but the parents themselves can be an obstacle in some cases. For example, a child who shows no interest in or talent for music should not be forced to take piano lessons because it pleases the parents. He or she should be allowed to do what is pleasing for *him* to do. People, even extremely young ones, are good at what they like to do. Methods and tools of learning should be supplied once a talent is recognized, but they cannot create a desire or talent that does not exist. Keep your child healthy, happy, loved, and well supplied, and he will find his own path to happiness and success according to his own potential.

In Michael's case, health appeared to be the initial problem, and after the difficulties associated with the colic had passed we were especially careful to watch for any behavioral changes that might indicate something wrong. Luckily, the only changes we saw were healthy and natural ones.

It's important to be aware of how a child develops, so that your well-meaning enthusiasm doesn't lead you to expect signs of growth that the child has not yet reached.

The following descriptions briefly illustrate the growth patterns of a child in various stages of development. Remember, however, that all children progress at their own individual rate according to the maturation process.

Four Months

By four months a child should have doubled his birth weight to about fifteen or sixteen pounds and have grown four inches or more. Physically, he can generally hold up his chest as well as his head when lying on the stomach. In a sitting position, he holds his head steady and carefully observes his surroundings. The average infant of this age can roll over from stomach to back and vice versa. Most can also reach for and grasp an object placed before him. In many ways, this is a period one wishes he would never outgrow. Self-discovery is beginning. The infant discovers his hands and fingers and spends minutes at a time watching them, studying their movements, bringing them together, and grasping one hand with the other. Also at this age nearly all babies smile, laugh, and coo quite selectively, much to the delight of doting adults. With all these treasurable memories tucked away, however, perhaps the most adorable part of a child at the age of four months, to which my wife and millions of other mothers can surely testify, is that he usually sleeps through the night. *All* of the night!

Eight Months

At eight months, babies have gained another four or five pounds and have grown about three inches. The hair is thicker and longer. The child probably has at least one tooth and perhaps as many as two or three. Most children at this age are able to get into a sitting position, and almost all can sit without support when placed in position. Occasionally a baby takes a few steps alone at this age, although it is generally too early for free walking. Most can stand while holding onto a supporting object and can sidestep around furniture to walk. However, the basic means of locomotion is still crawling.

From the time our son was eight months old he had a definite dislike for being on hands and knees. He wanted to walk, and nobody could tell him that he wasn't supposed to do so for another two or three months. He may have inherited my wife's looks, but the stubborn temperament is, unfortunately, all mine. Michael was what you would have to call a strong-willed child. Holding onto a chair, a sofa, my leg, or anything else within reach, he would pull himself into a standing position. After accomplishing this feat, however, he didn't quite know what to do next, so he simply let go—occasioning many bumps and bruises. At one point we were almost reluctant to take him out in public, for fear someone might think we were abusing him. So determined was he that at ten months he achieved his goal, almost a month earlier than the average child.

Anyone who spent an afternoon with Michael at that age could see that he was being all boy. Boys, more than girls, like to climb and explore anything they can manage to get onto with a good stretch.

At eight months all babies delight in filling both hands with objects and smashing them together if a pleasing noise is made. A cabinet or bottom drawer containing pots and pans is a likely and repeated target for discovery.

At this age the child is first learning to play. The play will become increasingly complex as he grows older, but peek-a-boo and patty-cake are pleasures that only a parent can appreciate. The only game I didn't enjoy was picking up an object my son had dropped so that he could drop it again and watch me pick it up and hand it to him again and again and again . . .

The most satisfying feeling that a child can give to a parent is that of being loved, needed, and special. Whether you're playing a game, taking him for a drive, or changing his diaper, an indescribable sense of closeness is created when you realize that the baby prefers your company over anyone's, except perhaps your wife's. To him, you and she are the world.

As a result of that family-centeredness, most babies experience what is called stranger distress. They become quite cautious and stare suspiciously at an unfamiliar face. If a stranger persists in attentions, the baby may burst into tears. His outstretched arms and tearful face as he reaches for you can give you an instant rush of pride: He wants only you. He wants his daddy.

Perhaps what astonished me most about my son at this age was the realization of how much he had grown in just a few months. One week he was a cuddly bundle in his crib, and the next thing I knew he was standing next to the bed trying to get my attention by eating the *TV Guide*. I felt as though next month he would be asking for the car keys.

Twelve Months

At one year the average infant weighs about twenty or twenty-one pounds and is twenty-eight or twenty-nine inches in height. Girls tend to be slightly smaller than boys, but remember, growth rates vary widely among babies.

Most infants at this age are trying either to walk or to utter their first words, but not both at the same time. Most achieve control of walking first, and then start talking. Those first words include "mama," "dada," "baby," "bye-bye," "hi," and the all-important "no."

As mentioned, at eight months babies begin to play with objects and people. They can throw small objects and begin to feed themselves with a spoon, with luck not at the same time. By twelve months they can actively manipulate their environment. They are able to undo latches, open cabinets, pull toys, and twist lamp cords. Their newly developed grasping ability with the thumb opposing the forefinger enables them to pick up grass, hairs, cigarette butts, and dead insects. They can turn on TV sets, explore kitchen cupboards, open casement windows, and poke things into electrical outlets.

Because children are so busy exploring their environment, parents and other care-givers must set limits to their research. They have to establish a balance between permissiveness and sufficient control to keep the baby safe. Of all the words a child knows at this age, "no" thus becomes the most important—and probably the most used word—for both parent and child.

As children enter their second year, they become more aware of themselves as persons separate from their parents and begin to exercise choice and preference. They may suddenly refuse a food that they have previously liked. They may protest loudly at bedtime, or they may engage in a battle of wills over a formerly routine event. They are fast approaching the Terrible Twos.

Eighteen Months

The eighteen-month-old, now usually called a toddler, weighs between twenty-two and twenty-seven pounds and is thirty-one to thirty-three inches in height. Almost all children at this age are walking alone. When they walk, they like to push or pull something with them or to carry something in their hands. Many of their actions are imitative, such as "reading" a magazine, sweeping the floor, or chattering on a toy telephone. Most can combine two words to make a simple sentence and can point to and name familiar objects. Watch them closely: They are growing fast!

Twenty-four Months

Run! Take cover! Man battle stations! The Terrible Twos are here. If we all had the energy that these two-year-olds show, I'm convinced that we could work three jobs and jog six miles afterward just for fun.

By the age of two, children can walk, run, skip, jump with both feet off the ground, ride a tricycle, kick a ball, climb steps, stack several building blocks, and accomplish a fairly good overhand throw of a ball. They crawl into, under, around, and over any object they choose. It is as if all the skills they have been developing and perfecting for two years have suddenly been mastered in a very short time span. Coupled with the explosive energy children possess at this age, they bear little resemblance to the helpless baby that came home such a short time ago. They have become inquisitive little people with well-defined personalities and their own way of doing things. Even roller skates won't help you to keep up with them, as they seem to be everywhere at once.

Since you will be working full time to support your family and will be away from home most of the day, pity your wife who has the "full-time job" of taking care of both you and the three-foot-tall, twenty-eight pounds of exploding dynamite. The following are some of the surprises I came home to find during my son's twelve-month reign of terror: twenty-two holes punched in the screening of our back porch by the axle of his toy truck; my potted plants uprooted, the dirt shaken off, and the plants stacked neatly behind the sofa; a full-size graffito drawn in Magic Marker on the back door; a large X marking the spot in indelible ink on five of my white shirts; and an endless list of objects thrown either into the fishtank or the toilet bowl.

One example of Terrible Twos enterprise was far from amusing. Michael liked to get up early in the morning and watch television before we arose. We thought nothing of it until one particular Sunday morning when my wife got up to fetch a bottle for our second son, Christopher. As she filled the bottle, she noticed an almost empty bottle of orange-flavored children's aspirin. Never underestimate the ingenuity of a child to get what he wants. The bottle had been on a shelf above the sink. Michael had dragged a chair all the way across the kitchen and climbed from it to the top of the counter to reach the bottle. To this day I have yet to figure out how he opened the child-proof cap—which defeats most adults. But one lesson is clear: It is not enough to keep medicines and poisons out of the reach of children; they must also be kept out of sight. Despite spending four days in the hospital, Michael suffered no lasting effects from the experience, but thousands of children each year are not so lucky. Remember, even though they are little people, they can get themselves into a lot of trouble. The best medicine a parent can give a child is thoughtful preventive medicine.

As was said earlier, your child's development during the first two years depends on the natural process of maturation and how well you meet his or her basic needs. The child must receive consistent care, adequate nutritious food and rest, must feel safe, and must have appropriate stimulating experiences to enable him or her to grow to the fullest potential. In short, you must give your child everything you yourself probably don't have at this point in your life.

The child is yours, and it is special because no one else of the nearly three billion people on this earth can make that claim. Use your brains, back, and soul to the best of your ability to take care of the family you've been granted. If you think for a moment that there's nothing special in the gift of a child to your wife and you, just ask a couple who have lost a child or are unable to have one. It may help you to understand how wonderful is the love of a child. A baby really does make a family as nothing else can.

CHAPTER 6

Families Forever, Drugs Never

As a teenage father, I trust that you have the motivation to make logical decisions in the best interests of yourself and your family. Drugs are an acknowledged threat to society as a whole, and the family—the "backbone" of society—in particular. This chapter focuses on the relationship between yourself as a young father and drugs, as regards two circumstances of contact: drug use itself, and the profitable distribution of drugs. The temptations, risks, rewards, and penalties for both are very great. Unfortunately, someone I knew didn't realize that in time and thus lost his own game of chance.

About a year after my friend John and I had graduated from high school, John decided to move in with a roommate, to share living expenses and perhaps be able to save some money. The roommate, Harry, was six or seven years older than John and more secure financially. He owned a new Firebird, wore fine clothes, and had an expensive stereo system, custom-made furniture, and other luxuries. Although I had been told that Harry had been out of work for some time, it never occurred to me to wonder how he had acquired such things; at eighteen one tends to look at the item itself and not what it takes to purchase it. I had no idea just how much money $14,000 was, but I could see and appreciate what it bought. I was naive in many other ways as well.

One evening I was invited to their apartment to play a few games of bumper billiards, drink beer, and watch "Saturday Night Live" on television (one of our favorite pastimes). While John and I were playing. Harry and two of his friends sat at a nearby table over a small pile of white powder, a straw, and some razor blades. John told me what was going on, and we decided to leave before the police arrived—if, in fact, the two men with Harry weren't undercover officers. Acting nonchalant, we put down our cues and calmly walked toward the door.

Once outside, we nearly fell over ourselves in a mad dash for my car parked down the street. My little Toyota never moved as fast as it did that night. It wasn't enough to leave the apartment; we left the city. Driving for fifteen or twenty minutes, we reached Ft. Lauderdale, where we roamed the streets for a couple of hours trying to decide whether it was safe for John to return home. When we did go back, the car driven by Harry's friends was no longer there, and we took the chance that there was no police stakeout waiting for us.

That was the last I saw of Harry, John, or their apartment for a number of weeks. Finally I decided to stop by unannounced one Saturday morning, and Harry answered the door. John wasn't home, so Harry and I began to talk. During the course of the aimless conversation, Harry did something that I will never forget. Probably to boast and show me how well his "business" was going, he unlocked a new safe that he had placed under the billiard table and produced a roll of money the likes of which I will probably never see again in my life. It consisted of $50s and $100s and was at least four inches in diameter: I was looking at some $40,000. I don't remember what I said, but it had to be something brilliant like "Wow!" I was making $60 a week at the time; what else could I have said?

Except for meeting Harry accidentally in a store where I was working, that was the last conversation I ever had with him. One day John told me that their apartment had been burglarized while they were both away; he commented on how strange it was that Harry's room had been ransacked but his own had not been touched. Soon afterwards, Harry started carrying a gun. Someone knew what was in that apartment, and John knew it was time to get out, which he did.

That was the last I heard of Harry until months later, when his picture appeared in a local newspaper with a caption reporting him missing. A friend had said that he had been working on a car with Harry when two men came by to pick Harry up. The friend didn't know who they were but said that Harry went willingly. Harry was never seen alive again. Two weeks later his body was found in a swampy field outside of town. Police labeled the killing as drug-related, and the coroner's report gave the cause of death as asphyxiation. His killers have never been found.

Dave, John, and I attended the funeral service for Harry. As it ended, Dave turned to me and said, "This never had to happen. Look at all the people who cared about him. There's no reason for him to be lying there dead." As the saying goes, "If you play with fire, you're going to get burned."

What surprised me most about the whole affair was that Harry came from a wealthy and influential family. He had no need of money, so why did he dig his own grave in search of it? There were many possible answers to that question, but all came down to bad judgment.

I ran across another example of bad judgment that led to catastrophe. A college friend of mine owns and operates a business that services and repairs aircraft engines. As in many businesses, people in the aircraft industry are known chiefly by their professional reputation. This friend told me of a man who had an established business at a nearby airport. With a fleet of three single-engine planes, he ran a successful courier service, flying passengers and packages to and from the Bahamas at a fee competitive with the major airlines. Unfortunately, however, the packages he brought to the United States on his return flights contained merchandise other than seashells and island rum, and one night upon landing in Florida he was arrested by customs officials. It seems that he had removed the rear seats from one of his planes and converted it into a kind of flying "pickup truck" carrying bales of marijuana. Under Florida law, his planes were confiscated, forcing his business to close down while he sat in jail awaiting trial, with bond set at $400,000, which he could not hope to raise. So much for flying high.

The purpose of these two stories is to show you actual examples of what can happen when "easy money" is earned by the sale or running of drugs. One man lost his business, reputation, property, and personal freedom.

The other lost his life. All for money that neither of them really needed.

When you are struggling and working as hard as you can just to make ends meet, life can be very frustrating. As some drugs sell for up to $300 per ounce, the temptation to earn apparently quick and easy money may be almost irresistible. You envision paying off those over-due bills and beginning to reach the life-style you've always wanted for yourself and your family.

To counterbalance that powerful lure, stop and think about what you have to gain and what you stand to lose. Weigh them carefully and you'll see an obvious im-balance.

A man who takes on a wife and a child while still in his teens must be practical, respected, and above all else responsible. Knowingly performing acts that are illegal violates all of those principles. Since you're reading this book, you must have an interest in coping with the problems of being a teenage father, and you're surely not going to risk the well-being of your family and yourself to reach for something illegally when in time it will present itself to you with no risks involved. Forget luck and chance. The only one hundred percent sure way to suc-cess is through hard work and patience. The hard work is in preparing for opportunities, while the patience comes in waiting for the right time and place to compete for the prize. Remember, compete only when *you* are ready.

I mentioned being left nearly speechless by the sight of $40,000 in cash. Although I'm not making quite that much yet, I'm making considerably more than I was at the time I saw it, and I'm well on my way to matching it in salary. It can be done, and I know it. More important than the money itself, however, is the fact that once I have earned it, I can enjoy it without having to worry about its being taken from me. Can a criminal, no matter how "successful," match that claim?

Also, forget the rationalization that you'll stop illegal transactions after "just one more time." Three of the basic human emotions are greed, more greed, and ultimate greed. There is no such thing as enough when it comes to large sums of money. If I can make $50 this week, maybe I can make $100 next week. Harry eventually paid the price of his own casket with the money he made. He finally did stop.

Harry will never again be anyone of importance or do anything ever again. Religious beliefs aside, that's what death means: the end, finished, no more. But the situation could have been worse. Harry paid for his mistakes with the only person he had, himself. No one's life depended on his bringing home the paycheck, no one needed him for protection, no one needed his guidance and decision-making. He had no family of his own to care for. No one. Perhaps if he had, he would have been more careful and been alive today.

You, with a family, stand to lose a lot more than Harry ever had to risk. As a father and a husband, you would be directly jeopardizing others who depend on you, for no justifiable reason. "Extra money," you say? Try again. Not too many other answers, are there? Okay, so now we have the answer: money. Did you ever hear of a part-time job? Retail stores have all sorts of wacky hours. How about security guard? Taxi driver? Telephone salesman? Gas station attendant? Just pick up the classified ads and look. Who knows, you might even find something you like better than your regular job.

If you are creative, why not use your spare time to produce works in metal or wood, draw, paint, write (there's one I never thought of), or grow plants (legal ones!). You'd be surprised at what art shows will exhibit and what people will pay money for.

If you're still not convinced of what I've said and the dangers involved in illegal drug trafficking, stop and think about how you'd feel toward a person who made it easier for your children to use harmful drugs. Then look yourself in the mirror and tell him what you think of him. For the sake of his own children and mine, I hope he listens.

I feel particularly strongly about the dangers of drug trafficking because I've seen people close to me step into the maze and find it difficult or impossible to find their way out. I was a very sheltered and naive teenager, but still I had many opportunities to become part of the drug scene both at school and at work. The possibilities for using drugs myself were even greater. Marrying and becoming a family man dispelled most of my naiveté and allowed me to see more clearly how much that scene actually surrounds us all.

Teenagers and people in general use recreational psychoactive drugs for two basic reasons: to escape something, and to be seen as fitting into a social set.

In seeking escape, they seek ways to relieve either societal pressures or boredom. It is their way of running without moving. Both escape and conformity seem to motivate teenagers, which would seem to account for their higher percentage of drug use. But escape is apparently the prime motivator as we grow older and take on adult responsibilities.

As a teenage father, you didn't have to grow older to

take on the responsibilities; they came with the title. In fact, pressure is probably the only thing that is not in short supply in your life at this time. You are under pressure to make enough money to pay the bills, to perform well at work, to keep your grades up if you're still in school, to be accepted by others, to be a good husband and father, pressure, pressure, PRESSURE!

Obviously, the only sure antidote is relaxation. However, somewhere along the line people have managed to convince themselves that the use of drugs will do the trick.

Drug Use Among High School Seniors

	Ever Used	*Daily Use*
Marijuana	60%	7.0%
Inhalants	12	0.1
Hallucinogens	13	0.1
Cocaine	17	0.3
Heroin	1	0.0
Other opiates	10	0.1
Stimulants	32	1.2
Sedatives	16	0.2
Tranquilizers	15	0.1
Alcohol	93	6.0
Cigarettes	71	20.3

As the chart shows, the three most popular drugs used to achieve that desired state of mind are alcohol, cigarettes, and marijuana.

Are you surprised by the first two? It's a fact that alcohol and nicotine (and caffeine) are drugs. To further test your knowledge, let me ask you another question. Assuming long-term use, which do you think would be more harmful to your body, alcohol or heroin? The answer may astonish you. Heroin actually is less damaging, because it leaves no permanent effects after use of the drug is stopped. Without treatment, withdrawal can be hell to live through, but body functions return to normal once the drug has passed through the system.

Alcohol, on the other hand, destroys gray cells in the brain and does irreversible damage to the liver, pancreas, stomach, and the entire gastrointestinal tract. It is linked to instances of cancer in the mouth and larynx. Severe alcohol withdrawal can, in fact, kill.

Now I'm not advising going out and buying nickel bags of heroin instead of a beer, but I do want to make clear that there are serious misconceptions and myths in the way people view drugs. Alcohol is the playtime, social indulgence, while heroin is the addictive killer, right? Or is it the other way around? Actually both statements are correct: Just ask an alcoholic. How we acquire our views depends on how society chooses that we should look at the two. Remember, there are no good or bad drugs, just good and bad ways to handle them.

Unfortunately, the bad way is too often accepted to obtain an effect that we consider good or desired. Drinking, in particular, is seen as a way to initiate conversation, make friends, or fit in with a crowd.

In our senior year in high school, my two friends and I made a virtual ritual of going out every Friday night and finishing off three or four six packs of beer in the space of four hours. We would go to the school football game and leave at half-time (our team was awful), play a few games of pinball, and get totally smashed.

When graduation came around and the party life was nearing an end, the situation began to worry me. I thought it over and asked myself one important question: Did I like the weekend drinking too much to give it up? I liked to believe that there was nothing about myself that I couldn't change or control if I really wanted to. It was a matter of personal pride that was put to the test. Luckily for me, I passed. Estimates of teenagers who can't pass that test and who become alcoholics range from 100,000 to 250,000 annually—and that represents only 2 percent of all alcoholics in the United States.

For three months after graduation, I drank nothing alcoholic—not a single glass of beer or wine. Thereafter I found no reason to resume drinking, and to this day I have only an occasional drink when it is offered to me. The pattern and the thrill were gone. I came to realize that the only reason I drank in the first place was to be accepted as part of the social set. At the time I thought it made me look mature and sophisticated. Once that particular social set was gone, so was my reason for drinking.

Remember, the time to take a drink is when you want it, not when you need it. There is nothing wrong with the great American pastime of watching a football game on a Sunday afternoon with a beer or two, or coming home from a hard day's work and grabbing a cold one from the refrigerator. The key is moderation. People tell themselves they need a drug, such as alcohol, to help them relax. That's all very well unless they make a habit of relaxing themselves into unconsciousness.

Having discussed the principal legal drug, let's look at the front runner on the illegal chart, which also holds third place among the most popular drugs in the country. I am referring to pot, grass, weed, or marijuana.

Marijuana is unlike alcohol and cigarettes in one important aspect: It is considered to be the "link point" or entry into the use of other illegal and much more dangerous drugs. Most marijuana users do not become users of other illegal drugs; however, those who do use other illegal drugs have usually tried marijuana first.

Marijuana use has never been proved to create significant health or personality problems. Users in the 1950s and early 1960s may have been seen to have serious personality problems as a group because at the time marijuana use represented a more deviant type of behavior. Some studies suggest that marijuana use at the high school level creates personality problems but that the same problems do not occur among college students. Why? Because it is not the student's use of the drug or a personality problem that changes dramatically after high school, but how his college peers and fellow students view his behavior.

Despite all governmental efforts, marijuana is still relatively easy to obtain. It may not cause the bodily harm of the use of alcohol or cigarettes, but the jail term it may bring can do serious damage to a career.

Only recently has science developed an encompassing and acceptable psychosocial definition of a person indulging in drug abuse. He or she is described as a person who uses drugs to such an extent, and in such a way, as to interfere with personal, social, or occupational behavior. Either drinking or taking drugs has long been recognized as a sign of serious trouble because it is an attempt to deny or hide a problem from oneself and others. It is essential for the person to understand the definition and, if it applies, to accept the fact that he does have a problem. Often that is half the battle of recovery, since a person cannot be treated until he wants to be.

The message of this chapter clearly is, "Don't use drugs, don't sell drugs, don't think drugs." But instead of merely preaching I hoped that showing you the evidence and the consequences of such actions would persuade you to make the right decision concerning yourself and your family.

For myself, I find that after spending nine or more hours a day at my job, the remaining time is precious to me and I refuse to waste it. I need it for working on my hobbies, enjoying physical exercise, playing with my kids, or doing a hundred other things I like to do. Using drugs on a regular or intermittent basis wastes time, energy, money, and—most of all—potential. Ultimately, it will rob you of your future and cripple you in your fight for survival. If you fail your family because of drugs, well, they don't call it "dope" for nothing.

CHAPTER 7

Wives Are People, Too

I t was brought to my attention—by my wife, of course—that very little in this book so far has dealt with the "copilot" of your marriage, your own wife.

How does the life you are trying to provide for her and your child look from her perspective? What does she see from her angle?

There's an old saying to the effect that you don't know how a man feels until you've walked a mile in his shoes. Sometimes the only way a person can appreciate someone else's point of view is to do just that, even if only figuratively.

My own lesson came when my wife was in the hospital for a week giving birth to our second child. It was necessary for me to stay at home and care for two-year-old Michael, which was all right with me, since I didn't particularly want to witness another Caesarean section. However, on the basis of that experience I am able to project what it would be like to be a housewife taking care of both a two-year-old and a husband. The following scenario involves a woman working to support the family and a househusband taking care of the home. I call it "A Day with Mr. Domestic." Don't fret, though; it's only for a day. One very long day.

The child is sick, and the husband has stayed up nearly all night walking, patting, and caring for the baby while his wife slept soundly. Morning finds him sleeping on the sofa, so as not to disturb his wife, with the baby lying restlessly beside him.

The alarm goes off at 7:30, slowly bringing the wife out of bed. Seeing her husband's bed empty, she goes into the living room and taps her husband on the shoulder.

"What are you doing out here?" she asks.

"The baby was crying during the night; didn't you hear him?"

"No, I slept like a rock. I'm going to go and take my shower."

The husband takes the child into the bedroom still asleep, then goes to cook his wife's breakfast and pack her a lunch to take to work.

"Breakfast is ready," he calls.

"I'm not finished yet," she answers, "can't you wait a minute?" She rambles through the apartment opening drawers and closet doors. "Where's my belt, have you seen it? Why is nothing ever where I left it?"

She picks up a pretty pink blouse from a hanger in the laundry room. "This will go nicely with my outfit. Hm, it needs to be ironed though. I wish you'd press my clothes right after you wash them," she says as she carries it into the kitchen. "Hurry, I'm almost late for work."

"All right, all right, I'll iron it. Sit down and eat your breakfast before it freezes over."

"Always with the smart remarks," she replies. "You wouldn't last twenty minutes hurrying over a job with a boss standing over you. This skirt could use touching up, too; it's kind of wrinkled at the hem."

She takes off the skirt and hands it to her husband, ready with the iron in his hand. Sitting at the table in her slip, she prepares to eat. "You broke my yolk! You know I can't eat an egg once the yolk is broken."

"I'll fix another one for you; don't be so impatient," he says.

"Never mind, I'll just have toast and finish this cup of coffee. Maybe I'll grab a doughnut on the way to work," replies the wife.

"Your clothes are ready."

"Good, I'm almost late." She quickly dresses and goes to brush her teeth. Upon returning, she opens her purse, pushes the contents from side to side, and finally begins to remove everything piece by piece. "Where are my keys?"

"The baby was playing with them. You left them on the television set for him to reach again," says the husband.

"Well, why didn't you take them away from him? Now I've got to hunt for them." She briefly scans the room without moving a step. "There they are on the floor." She picks them up. "Give me a kiss, I've got to go."

"Don't forget your lunch," he reminds her.

"I won't."

The baby begins to cry in the bedroom.

"The baby's awake again, by the way. See what you can do for him." She thinks to herself as she leaves, "Why does there always have to be so much aggravation here in the morning?"

As the day continues, the husband faces his usual barrage of chores. The baby has to be fed, his clothes changed, his medicine given, and a safe way to amuse him found. These are tasks that are done routinely throughout the day. Now he can start to work. First he must finish ironing the clothes as his wife had asked, start another load of the endless pile of laundry, wash the breakfast dishes, vacuum the carpets, do the grocery shopping, and feed the baby his lunch. Then he's ready to have his own lunch, which usually lasts a whole ten minutes if he's lucky.

After lunch he cleans up the mess the baby made on the floor, table, and himself. His wife calls from work during her lunch hour, as usual, to tell him how much she hates her boss, her job, and life in general. After this cheery conversation, the afternoon continues with washing the lunch dishes, hanging the laundry to dry, telling innumerable salesmen that they must speak with the woman of the house, who makes all the decisions. Putting the baby down for his nap, he catches the necessary hour of "Guiding Light" while folding laundry.

After starting preparations for dinner, he goes in to check on his son, who should still be sleeping soundly. Instead he finds the baby has crawled out of his crib and is amusing himself throwing various objects into the toilet bowl to watch the splash. Retrieving that situation, and establishing the baby with things to occupy his mind and hands, the husband continues to set the table for dinner. His preparations are nearly complete and the roast is ready to come out of the oven when the phone rings.

"I still have a few things to do here, so I'll be about a half hour late getting home," says his wife.

"I wish you could have told me sooner," says the husband. "Everything's almost ready."

"I didn't know until a few minutes ago. I'll be home soon."

"All right," he replies resignedly, "I'll try to keep your dinner warm."

The wife walks in the front door at quarter past six, a full forty-five minutes past the time she had told him over the phone.

"Damn job, I don't know how much longer I can take it. I tell you, today was the worst I can remember."

Purse, keys, and hair clips are placed on top of the TV set. Blouse and belt are thrown over the back of a chair. Her shoes are tossed off into a corner of the living room as she storms past her husband to the bedroom to change into blue jeans and a T-shirt.

"I was so busy I couldn't even think straight half the day. On top of all that, they put some bozo above me who had to ask *me* about procedure. He's probably making twice the money I do, and he's asking me how to do things. What a joke! I'd laugh if it wasn't so stupid."

"Sit down and have something to eat," says the husband.

"I'm not that hungry; I'll just have some potatoes. Where's the paper?"

"It's over by the TV."

She gets the newspaper and opens it on the table next to her as she begins to eat.

"I want to go to my cousin's house tomorrow to help him sort out some of the mess in his garage," he says. "Is that all right with you?"

"This group made over four million off of one record. One record!"

"Did you hear what I said?"

"Yeah."

"What did I say?" asks the husband.

"Huh? I don't know. Leave me alone; I'm reading the paper."

"I asked you if I could go to my cousin's house tomorrow."

"Fine, why do you need my permission?"

"Because if I didn't make sure you heard me, you'd get all upset if you called tomorrow and I wasn't home," he says. "So can I go?"

"Sure, as long as the house is clean," replies his wife.

"What difference does that make? You never notice when it's clean, only when it's dirty so you can yell at me."

"I'm tired," she says. "I don't want to talk about it any more." She glances at the baby smearing food on his face. "I think he's finished eating. I'm going in the living room."

The husband takes the baby from his chair and cleans him up. He clears the table, does the dishes, gives the baby his bath and puts him to bed, all before his wife has finished watching an episode of "Star Search." Her only useful act was to get herself a can of soda from the refrigerator. He finally sits down to rest.

"That guy's got a nice rear end," says the wife.

"If I ever said something like that about a good-looking woman on TV, I'd never hear the end of it," he thinks, not daring to say it aloud. "We'd fight for hours."

"Now that the baby's asleep, maybe we can have a little tumble," she says.

"Not now; I don't feel like it. Besides, I thought you were tired?" he responds.

"I suddenly feel refreshed."

"Maybe later."

"Never mind, I'll just have to do without again. I wouldn't want to put you to any trouble," she says sarcastically. "A woman works hard all day to support her family, something you know nothing about, and she can't even get a little affection from her husband when she comes home. There are plenty of guys at work that wouldn't mind that job."

"Well, maybe you should get it from them!" he says as he storms from the room.

She gets up to change the TV channel as if nothing has been said. "Aggravation," she says to herself. "Always aggravation."

Much of the dialogue spoken by the working woman in this skit probably sounds familiar, doesn't it? How does it feel to receive it as a male "housewife"? How would you like the job full time? No pay, long hours, little job satisfaction, no opportunity for advancement, and probably worst of all a demanding and temperamental "boss." Try recruiting a worker on the basis of those untempting working conditions.

As recently as thirty or forty years ago, housewife may have been the ideal occupation for American women, but times do change. During World War II women were needed in factories to keep up production for essential industries while the men were fighting overseas. After the war, understandably, they were reluctant to go back to the kitchen.

Since many two-income families need the wife's paycheck just to survive, the working woman has proved to be a healthy trend in today's high-cost society. But financial gain is not the only consideration. It is a great asset to a woman's personal pride and self-image to be known as more than simply "Mr. Smith's wife." A woman wants to be a woman in her own right and known for her own qualities, not those of her husband. Only a very weak and insecure man would consider this desire to be a threat. Two people working toward the same goals make those goals easier to achieve.

The job of housewife (and mother) must be recognized as a tough and important occupation for the well-being of a family. Your own job is both tough and important, yet it cannot become your sole purpose in life. By the same token, housework cannot be your wife's only reason for living.

Some women choose to throw themselves wholeheartedly into the task of keeping their home spotless and organized and their husband happy. If they are content with the housewife's role, fine. As a husband, however, don't think you're doing her any favors by putting her in that position if she doesn't want to be there. You'll suffer the consequences later when she resents you for "locking her in."

A person cannot be a possession. If your wife's only achievements in life are those that you, as the husband, provide, your wife won't have much to take pride in other than her children.

Sometimes, in fact, the children are all the wife has. As a result, she becomes overprotective—which ultimately harms the children.

Without question, a wife's family does come first, but it need not be her only interest or accomplishment. A wife, like any human being, has many talents and interests that should be exploited. To restrict her potential would be as foolish as restricting your own. A family, like any structure, is only as strong as its component elements. The stronger the components, the more solid the structure. Remember, it is easier to be a success in the world once you are a success at home.

You may wonder if I, as a husband, practice what I preach. Well, believe me, I am doing all I can to avoid what I call the "forty-year syndrome" in my marriage. When my wife is forty years old, I don't want her to look back at her youth and see what she could have been "if only" or could have done "if only." The blame for those missed opportunities would undoubtedly center on me. My goal is to have fewer problems as I grow older, not more, and my solution is simply to make sure my wife has all her chances.

After we were married, my wife decided to quit her job and devote her time to caring for the baby. I agreed, since I strongly believe that a child's place is with his mother and the father's responsibility is to earn a living for his family. Once our second son is of school age, however, those circumstances will change.

For that reason, I insisted that, to prepare for that day, my wife take classes at the community college, working toward a degree. She has already earned her GED equivalency certificate and is looking forward to going back to school. Who knows, perhaps she'll earn a law degree someday and will support me! Not really, though. I couldn't stand the life of a househusband.

The most important thing to remember is to think twice before throwing a husband's most frequent remark at your wife. Don't accuse her of not working! The name of the game is appreciation. Like love, give it and you'll get plenty in return. Wives, after all, are people too.

CHAPTER ◇ 8

Looking Forward to
Looking Back

During my first year of marriage, the title of this chapter would have seemed absurd. Dinners of macaroni and cheese two or three times a week because it was all we could afford may not be the best of memories, but it makes me appreciate all the more the occasional steak we can now enjoy. In fact, it is somehow made tastier by the knowledge that I can have something that was once beyond my reach for myself and my family.

Looking back in this regard is a pleasant task. The happy sound of my younger son giggling in his sleep tells me that I have done well so far not only financially, but also in what is happening before my eyes. All four of us are growing up in our own way. My wife and I certainly aren't the same people we were four years ago, and my sons have already changed from babies to little boys. Can seeing them as older boys, teenagers, and young adults be far away?

True, they would follow that progression of growth even without me, but their short past, their present, and their long future would certainly be different. They might well be facing a strange, threatening, and inhospitable world that neither children nor adults should have to see. However, adults created it, and they can change it, or at least their own little corner of it, if they so desire.

I have created a stable home with a loving and caring family. That is my reality and my pride. If I am able to teach my children by example today, tomorrow they will grow up and perhaps build families of their own on the same model. Nothing, including people, can be built without a strong foundation. If I am successful at this important responsibility as the nominal head of our household, I will be directly and indirectly responsible for three or more solid corners of family life.

Here I am talking about grandchildren already! Somehow, the thought doesn't seem so distant anymore. The three or four premature gray hairs that I pull out every month or so tell me that the time is already on its way. Everyone grows old; some sooner than others, regardless of time.

That is especially true when speaking of a person's level of maturity. A teenage father must be older than his chronological age if he is to survive. Society expects that, the family that depends on him expects it, and, most important, he expects it of himself. Life is speeded up through necessity.

Although most men don't become fathers until they are in their late twenties or early thirties, a young father must cope with the same pressures and responsibilities despite the ten-year age difference. Since time equals experience in most matters, a father at seventeen or eighteen is at a comparable disadvantage. He must learn to behave, think, and deal with life like an older man.

The situation produces an unexpected side effect that can best be described as similar to adolescent "growing pains." Mentally the young father is no longer a teenager, but by the same token he cannot be the thirty-year-old man he is expected to be. He can mature and develop much faster than those his own age, but he cannot fully overcome the ten years of life that he has yet to experience. For that reason he may feel especially awkward both with people his own age and with those whom he is striving to emulate and surpass.

That was my own situation for quite a long time; however, recently I have begun to notice a change. It becomes increasingly easy to relate to those around me. The personalities of those of my own age are changing rapidly as they grow older. At twenty-three, most of them are now thinking along the lines of stability that I was seeking at nineteen. They and I are entering a sort of "catch-up" phase. In maturity they are catching up to me as I am gaining on the thirty-year-old age group—all through the passage of time. Happily, some problems still solve themselves. Not many, but some.

That "head start" of mine did have some definite advantages, but like everything else, one must take the good along with the bad. Being forced to grow up quickly makes a capable person much more aware of his environment and increases his ability to deal with a wider range of situations and problems; that, in turn, enables him to excel. Unfortunately, that added awareness carries a heavy price. Time that was once spent dating, going to the beach, partying with friends, or other activities of the easy life must be forfeited to work and the necessities of survival. A lot of immediate enjoyment is given up for future benefit. When you're traveling the highway of life at eighty miles an hour, you're ahead of the pack but you're not seeing much of the scenery.

I'm banking, however, on the proposition that hard work now will bring more than average leisure later, after we've won the race. After all, I'll be only forty-two when my youngest son turns twenty, if we stick to our decision to have no more children. At that time, with my wife pursuing her chosen career, my sons ready to go out on their own, and me earning a good income in a desired field, life will be easy again. That is a promise I have made to myself. It is for the well-being of my family and this specific end that I work.

That will be my life as I see it for myself. Of course, tomorrow I could step in front of a bus and write finis to all my plans, but going Greyhound in that manner isn't what I have in mind. On the other hand, someone else's plan might be just to muddle through with the least possible effort. Life is different things to different people. It is what you make it; it's a learn-as-you-play kind of game. To win, you must understand the rules and observe them in the way that works best for you. The final prize is yours to award.

After surviving the first rough turns at the board while still inexperienced, you'll find the game becomes easier as you go along. Never simpler, but certainly easier to play as you grow accustomed to its twists and surprises. Turns pass faster and faster until the end is reached and the game is over—for you. Your children, however, are several turns behind and must complete their game, as will your grandchildren and great grandchildren in time. As you race through the game and that "highway of life," slow down to appreciate those who are following you; for whatever life is, it is not forever.

Looking up at the bookshelf beside my desk, I see works by such writers as Mark Twain, William Faulkner, Herman Melville, and William Shakespeare. (For present purposes, we'll overlook the two Jim Davis paperbacks of *Garfield*.) All of those men—except Davis—are dead and gone, yet today I can read their thoughts and enjoy their style simply by opening a book at any page of my choice. The books are products of their minds. The mind is, after all, the essence of a person's personality and being. Therefore, a very large part of those men lives on without the constraints of time or age. However, no words in a book, no old photographs or even images in a motion picture can really make one "live" again as is possible in the memory and dreams of others. It is our wives and children, our family and friends who hold the secret to a continued existence after we are gone. Ironically, then, even though our mind is the essence of our being, we can live on only in the minds and hearts of others.

If life as remembered is better than present reality, which is actually the more desirable? It's a hard question to answer. You've heard the expression, "It's better to be remembered as I was, not as I am."

My grandfather must be well aware of that, even if he cannot express it. A series of strokes over the past thirteen years has slowly robbed him of even the most basic control of his body. He cannot walk or speak. His only means of communication is hand gestures, although one can tell that his mind is sharp and alert inside that useless body. Perhaps that is why people refer to such conditions as "living death," He is imprisoned in silence.

Earlier I explained my understanding of life. This is death. Everything is tightly locked inside him, never to be revealed or shared with others. How pitifully easy my struggles and hardships with life seem, compared to his. All that he has left are memories of his youth when he was a complete person with the world before him. How would he answer my question? How would you?

A person's future, as well as what will become his past, is determined by what he does *now*. Regardless of circumstances, a person who does not work to fulfill himself now will have nothing either in front of him or behind him.

That premise is the basis for what men and women experience as the "mid-life crisis," the depressing belief that people often acquire in their forties that, having arrived at the halfway point in life, they have no appreciable future or noteworthy past. Such a belief can drastically alter one's behavior and cause severe emotional strain if it is not overcome.

Here, too, however, a young father carries a special immunity. Raising a family and enduring many trials and experiences at an early age creates especially strong ties to the past as well as to the future. Thus, the dreaded crisis may be anticipated as nothing more serious than a brief discomfort.

Sadly, many young people never even make it to the midpoint in their life. Tens of thousands of teenagers each year choose to become a memory through suicide, and the number is increasing. It is heartbreaking because of the enormous waste of energy and talent, but it is a fact. Extreme depression along with inability to deal with the heightened pressures of the teenage years is cited as the major cause of youthful suicide.

Earlier I said that in my view death is when we are no longer able to express ourselves to others in a meaningful and fulfilling way. A teenager contemplating suicide is suffering the same absence of communication, but rather than not being able to reveal his feelings to others, he feels than no one is willing to listen. Too many people want to shape and mold his mind and personality, and too few are willing just to stop and listen to the efforts of all that conditioning. Life apparently becomes tortuous and incomprehensible, and people naturally dislike the things in life that they don't understand. If the communication gap continues long enough, the teenager simply decides to give up.

Even under pressures that are greater than "normal," however, very few teenage parents take this desperate out. First, whether or not they really like it, they have a mate with whom they can discuss problems and communicate on a personal basis. Second, they have a child, in whom they have a vested interest and a purpose for the future. That's what I call a real lease on life. There is none better. A child strengthens one's life and one's relationship with others.

If there is anything in the concept of immortality, it must lie exclusively in one's children and descendants. That is their ultimate gift to us. One of my sons has "my" eyes and hair, while the other has my nose and temperament; but when I am gone both will carry my memory as well as these remnant features of myself into the future, as I carry my father's and his father's before him. Genealogically, that is as close to "living" immortality as a human being can come.

Even that thought, however, has its drawbacks. Probing far enough back into one's own roots might, I suspect, be quite interesting, if not shocking. Going back ten or twelve generations, would we find a famous general, a world statesman, or a horse thief who was tarred and feathered before being hanged? Perhaps we'd rather not know. If we're able to be ourselves and have the selflessness to let our children do the same, immortal or not, that's what counts in the long run.

To conclude this chapter on looking forward to looking back, here's an incident that exemplifies what it can in fact mean to some people. Recently I was accompanying a fellow worker on his sales rounds. As we drove, we began to talk about ourselves and our college years. Idle chatter, really, until he began to describe his relationship with a girl he had known during his senior year. He is a man who likes to boast about his "conquests," but it struck me as odd that he revealed none of that attitude as he spoke of this particular girl: only how she looked, how she talked, and what fun they had together. He told me how she had had two abortions, because they loved each other but weren't ready for marriage. He was twenty-two then. Now, at thirty, his views were changing. I listened quietly but could not give him the sympathy I felt he was seeking. He said sadly that today he could have been the father of two children, one seven years old and the other eight. Perhaps boys, with whom he could go into the yard and toss a football.

"You've got two boys, haven't you?" he asked.

"Yeah, one's three and the other's year and a half," I replied. "They race each other to the door when I get home. Each wants to be first to say hello to Daddy."

I had several caustic comments in mind but thought it better to let him continue to do the talking. There's a time for being callous and a time for being cautious. I'd learn more about his viewpoint that way, and get to know the feelings of a man who gave up the chance for a family—twice in this case. Perhaps it was cruel, but I wanted to continue the conversation to force him to think about this past, possibly painful, relationship. I had to be careful not to say the wrong things, however, or appear too condemning (or condoning) on such a sensitive subject, or I might cause permanent bad feelings between us. Surprisingly, however, he was almost as interested in finding out about me as I was about him. I was doing what he could not, and it somehow fascinated him. He, in fact, asked me more questions than I had a chance to ask him. So I became content to watch and listen to his responses to my remarks.

"You must have been really young when you got married," he said. "How old were you?"

"Nineteen."

"That was too young. What did your parents say when you told them your plans?"

"What could they say? They were upset at first, but they got used to the idea. Now they'd probably want my head on a platter if I were ever to talk about divorce. They're very traditional people. Besides," I explained, "every parent wants to be a grandparent. For them it just came sooner than expected."

"Did you live with them for a while, or did you go right out and find a place of your own?"

"We lived with them for six months. We were crowded into one room, and the arrangement was kind of awkward for a while, but no big deal really. My parents helped us get our own apartment, since housing isn't exactly affordable when you're making four dollars an hour."

"No, I guess not," he said. "Does your wife work?"

"No, I'm kind of old-fashioned. Maybe it's my up-bringing, with my own mom never working, but I think one parent should be at home with the children. Some-one besides a baby-sitter has to guide children and answer their questions as they grow up. Until they reach school age and have a strong background, I won't trust anyone with that responsibility besides my wife and myself."

"Didn't that make things really tough? I mean, I'm sure you could have used a second paycheck. How did you manage?"

"You do what's necessary to survive," I replied. "Some things had to be sacrificed."

I was pleased with this all-purpose answer.

"I was never good at doing without things," he said. "I was making $25,000 a year before I even moved away from home."

"What were you making when you considered marry-ing your girlfriend?" I asked cautiously.

"Nothing. I was working in my father's cleaning store for an allowance at the time." Perhaps anticipating my next question, he continued, "I offered to help her support the baby, both times. She didn't feel it was right to have them and not be married." He began to breathe rather heavily between sentences. "The second time I really felt terrible, you know what I mean?"

I didn't know what to say.

"She was so sweet," he said. "I didn't want her to do

it; it wasn't even my idea. Thinking back on it, we really should have got married and at least tried to make it."

I noticed a strong tone of regret.

"You don't have to justify anything to me. I'm not God," I answered. "But let me ask you this. You sound as though you both were really in love. What stopped you from getting married? Two people in love with a baby on the way seems to me to be as good a reason as any."

"Neither of us are very responsible people," he answered. "We didn't think we could handle it. That's why I'm a salesman today, peddling office equipment, just like you."

I felt a note of sarcasm in his voice. "Certainly NOT like me," I thought. I remembered my fourth-grade teacher's favorite phrase, "If you can't say anything nice, don't say anything at all." Happily, we arrived at our next stop before there was time to say much more. But what nearly floored me was the remark he made as we were about to step out of the car.

"You know," he said, turning toward me, "you know a lot about the situation of being a very young father. From your own experience, maybe you should write a book."

I almost broke down and told him that was exactly what I was doing, but thought better of it. To tell him that he had just completed my final chapter seemed unwise.

"Maybe I will," I said. "Maybe I will."

It's unfortunate that there are so many people like my co-worker, who don't have the will or the courage to change their life, or even to try to change it, for the better. Not even willing to try, that's the real shame. They have no motivation and no self-confidence, which is the companion of courage.

What seems so strange is that it is usually this type of person, with a defeatist attitude, who does most of the grumbling and complaining about things in general. To them, everything is flawed, but few of them are willing to do anything to improve it. Most of them sit out their lives waiting for the pot of gold to fall into their waiting lap. That attitude is just as unrealistic as our credit card mentality.

To obtain anything worthwhile or important, we must work to earn the chance and the opportunity to get it. It's true there is no such thing as something for nothing. People won't make opportunities for you; you have to earn them by doing the best you can and hoping it's good enough. As a family man, three or more people are counting on your efforts.

The vast majority of people never achieve any of the goals that are important in their lives. That is for two basic reasons: They don't know exactly what they want, and they don't know how to get it. First, their goals are ill-defined, totally out of reach at the moment, or too many, thus dividing their energies. Before you loose an arrow, you must have a single target in your sights. Second, people who do have a reachable goal tend to falter in confusion and frustration, being unable to make or recognize progress in their efforts. They tend to see their goals in blind desire, while neglecting opportunities that could forward them if seized in time. Thus, close observation and analysis could reveal achievements and failures, making it possible to revise methods accordingly. By recording one's weekly or monthly progress toward a goal (as one would do in body-building or dieting), one is less likely to become discouraged, and one's persistence can pay off.

As a young father, persistence in what you are attempting can only lead to a bounty of success. You have more, not less, going for you than the average person. If you don't believe that, go back to page one and start over again. But remember that you won't believe anyone else until you believe in yourself. Persistence in that is perhaps the most important of all things considered. If you have confidence in your own abilities, whatever your goals may be, like a fast runner you're off to a good start.

Throughout this book I have strongly stressed certain values: love, care, faith, strength, and pride. Those are words of such infinite meaning that any attempt to define them, even from my own single perspective, seems futile. My purpose has been not to define these thoughts or emotions, but simply to relate them to you, the reader, from the point of view of a young father. This book tells of how I see the world and what I have learned out of my own experiences. It is my own way of looking back, and looking ahead. Like life, it is sometimes serious and sometimes silly. I have tried to be as honest as possible in expressing my feelings and opinions. If what I have said helps anyone to realize and appreciate the situation of a teenage father, or sets an example for someone in a similar situation, then my efforts will have been truly worthwhile.

I've always liked books that have a happy ending, and mine will be no exception. To the young fathers of the world, I leave one last thought. After all is said and done, when you see that young face smiling at you and calling you Dad, occasionally (not always, but occasionally) you'll realize that it all wasn't so bad after all. My good wishes as a fellow parent and a peer go with you on your journey.

P A R T ◇ 2

CHAPTER ◇ 9

Help on the Way

I have told you my story, describing the difficulties
and how I dealt with them, all the way down to the
ultimate resolution. But you should remember that
my solution was applied directly to my own circumstances. It is more than likely that your situation is
different from mine, and perhaps different in the extreme. In that case, my methods may not work for you,
although the attitudes (resilience, cooperation, fortitude,
determination) will work for everybody. Each particular case will feature different faces, different places,
and a wide variety of emotions. The only thing we have
in common is that we have a heavy burden to deal with,
and dealing with it is not easy.

According to the June, 1985, issue of *Psychology
Today*, there are more than two million unwed teenage
fathers in this country. Add to that the married teenage
fathers, and you have a core group of teens who have to
face seemingly impossible odds. The obstacles that confront that teenage father are some of the toughest chal-
lenges that any minority in America has to face.

It is extremely important to recognize that you are

part of a minority, and your minority is one of the most ignored and maligned minorities in the country. Your age, financial status, and sex combine into a formidable triple whammy; those are three nasty strikes against you. But while you should be aware that you are a member of a minority, you should also recognize that you are not alone, that somebody out there has discovered your plight and developed programs that can help you.

I am convinced that the person who can help you the most is the mother of your child. You won't be able to raise the child by yourself, and there is no good reason to believe that she would have it any easier. As parents working together, you can depend on each other for support in times of need, financially and emotionally. It takes two to make a child, and it takes two to raise that child so that the youngster can reach his or her potential.

If you had made your baby in paradise, the solution would be simple. It would be just you two in endless springtime, plenty of food for the picking, and no interference. But you are no doubt aware by now that you made your baby in neither a paradise nor a vacuum, and you're bound to run into plenty of interference, if you haven't already.

Every single instance of teenage pregnancy (estimates range from 500,000 to one million) comes equipped with its own set of circumstances. If there is one common thread that runs through all of those situations, it is the emotion that they generate: outrage. A young girl with a big belly drives most adults right up the wall with anger and disgust, and that seething anger is seldom directed at the pregnant girl. The startling picture of a pregnant girl usually induces sympathy and pity for her, while the rage is reserved for the evil, footloose young man who is

responsible. Even in this tolerant time, an unmarried
pregnant teenager is still a symbol of disgrace and
spoiled innocence, and the American public has little
sympathy for the man who plucked her virtue. The social
position of the teenage male in question does little to
help his cause:

> Typically, they [teenage fathers] are out of school
> and out of a job and ashamed of their helplessness as
> a parent. If they try to help, they usually are not
> welcomed by the girl or the parents, who "feel he's
> caused enough problems."[1]

That is one stunning barrier that I did not have to confront. It is hard enough to deal with an unexpected pregnancy and the inevitable changes it will bring to your life
without having to deal with irrational opposition from
your girlfriend's parents. I still think that marriage is the
best possible beginning to a solution, but don't forget
that the girl's parents may not want her to marry a guy
who has "caused enough problems."

Cliff and Sandy were all of fifteen years old when
Sandy became pregnant. Cliff was scared, but optimistic:
"I dreamed about how good things could be—how we'd
get married and I'd be a father. I knew it wouldn't be
easy, but I could get a job at the mill, and we could live on
my family's farm. I just knew that somehow we'd make it."

Cliff's optimism was admirable, but the road to his
family's farm was long, with plenty of roadblocks along
the way.

---

[1] Van Biema, David, *People Weekly*, 12/1/86, pp. 81–82.

Sandy's mother and father, however, "wouldn't listen to anything we had to say and kept asking how she let this happen. They told her what a no-good creep I was," Cliff lamented. "Then, after a long argument, they told me to get out and stay away from their daughter."

Later, Cliff learned that Sandy's parents had taken her to a nearby town for an abortion and had sent her to another state to live with relatives. "I couldn't believe it! Sometimes I get real angry that nobody asked me what I thought needed to be done. I don't think I'll ever get over it."[2]

The crucial time period between conception and birth is fraught with passion, tough decisions, tension, heightened emotions, and wild reversals in loyalty. In many cases, the teenage mother's family forms a thorny cocoon around the girl, and they exercise both their legal power and the power of parental persuasion to keep the teenage father at a "safe" distance.

Cliff received a sudden and harsh education at the tender age of fifteen; as if dealing with the pregnancy weren't enough, he was also insulted, excluded, and ignored as Sandy's parents aborted his child and removed Sandy from his life. Perhaps the hardest lesson of all was that a well-meaning teenage father who admits his mistake and aspires to make good can wind up despised and utterly powerless.

Hal Warden's ordeal is equally sobering and well documented. Hal became something of a celebrity

---

[2] Robinson, Bryan, *Psychology Today*, December 1985, pp. 60–70.

when, at age twelve, he impregnated his fifteen-year-old playmate Wendy Chapell while he and his family were in Alaska. When Hal's family moved back to their hometown in Tennessee, Wendy sprang the good news to Hal over the phone. Wendy joined Hal and his family in the Lower 48, where they were married. "You've never seen two people more in love," said Hal's father.

The rice had barely hit the pavement when Wendy's mother flew to Tennessee to charge Hal's father with kidnapping her daughter. Wendy talked her mother out of leveling the charge, but a month later Wendy crumbled and fled back to Alaska. Hal filed for divorce. Wendy returned to Tennessee, afraid that she would lose custody of the unborn child if she didn't return.

When the baby, named Heather, was born, TV's *Hour Magazine* flew the joyous couple to Hollywood to relate their tale of young love and parenthood. The Tokyo Broadcasting System flew them to Japan for more of the same.

Hal and Wendy paid a Christmas visit to Wendy's family in Alaska. Once there, says Hal, Wendy's mother threw him out and persuaded Wendy to stay. Hal was awarded the divorce, on grounds of cruel and inhuman treatment, but he lost the battle for custody of the child. Hal is allowed to see his daughter twice a year. "There's just no justice in the world," said Hal.[3]

Whenever I feel sorry for myself because I can't go out and hang loose with my pals anytime I feel like it, or I can't blow my paycheck on a new compact disc because I've got a wife and kids who need a roof and hot meals, I

---

[3] *People Weekly*, 9/23/85, p. 43.

think about Cliff and Hal and count my blessings, slowly, thrice.

When you consider the deck stacked against the teen-age father, and that father is you, and yet you've had your child and your woman is with you, you must realize how fortunate you really are. If you've run up against some of the barriers that Cliff and Hal slammed into, though maybe not as extreme, you will no doubt share their sense of injustice. Let's face it, teenagers are not equipped to deal successfully with legal and social injustice, and nobody seems in a big hurry to help them out.

Two distinct trends are on the rise that will provide some solace to those of you who have suffered a crisis as Cliff and Hal did. Both trends are a result of increasing tolerance in the late eighties.

The first and most important hurdle for the teenage father is to assure himself that he will not only be a father, but a father who will be able to share in the duties of raising his child. Though the issue of abortion is hotly debated in the United States, it is evident that the majority of abortions performed are not on teenage mothers. *Children Today Magazine* published the re-sults of research done by the Child Welfare League of America. The CWLA study focused on mothers under the age of sixteen years and followed their development over a two-year period. Eighty-five percent of the mothers were black, eleven percent were white, three percent American Indian, and one percent Hispanic.

Only one third of the mothers said they had *consid-ered* abortion, while only one fifth said they had thought seriously about relinquishing their babies for adoption. All of the mothers kept their babies.[4]

Judy Folkenburg takes this development a step further in the May 1985 issue of *Psychology Today* (p. 16):

> Not only has society become more accepting of the unwed mother, but according to survey data, the girls' families strongly opposed adoption as an alternative. "Despite almost universal verbal disapproval [of adoption], some girls had in fact considered it, but the resultant community and familial pressures against it were so pervasive that they were unable to carry through with their plans," say the researchers.

The information means that your baby stands an excellent chance of being carried to term, and since more teen mothers are declining to give the baby up for adoption, there is an even greater chance that yours will remain with the woman with whom it was conceived. You have a chance. There is hope. Just getting to the point where your baby breathes the same air as you is a major achievement. But, as Lynn Langway writes in *Newsweek* (October 24, 1984), "More and more of these youngsters [teenage mothers] decide to keep their children, rather than put them up for adoption, [but] fewer are marrying the males responsible."

Now, it is extremely important that you don't let statistics spook you. Try to remember that in almost

---

[4] Miller, Shelby, *Children Today*, May/June 1984, pp. 26–29.

every case there is at least one person who has beaten the odds, against whom all the failures are measured. I have no statistics to prove what I am about to declare, but I'll lay serious money that even in the smallest percentage, *especially* in the smallest percentage, the guy who succeeds against the odds is one tough young man, someone who is not afraid of hard work.

I know a few people who are afraid of hard work. They prefer to be in the majority, normal, average. To them, it is a challenge to be ordinary. But if you are a teenage father, you had better realize that you are gone out of that league, you just lost your membership in the Ordinary Joe Club. You're special, like it or not.

The mother of your child may have parents who don't think you're too special. Let's face it, the *mother* may not be all that pleased with you either. And there's a good chance that your own kid screams like a smoke alarm whenever you try out the cootchie-coo. You could be in for a lot of blame and abuse. Remember Cliff and Hal. That's why you have to remind yourself that you're special; nobody else is going to. That's why you have to be strong. One thing that you don't have to be is married.

As far as I was concerned, getting married right away was the best step for me to take with my wife and my unborn child, because all of us, including our families, were willing. There was no time left to postpone maturity. But I was not as young as some teenage parents, and there is a big difference between nineteen years of age and fifteen years, especially when marriage is the issue.

Marriage may not be right for you. It depends on your age, which translates into employability. Another factor is your level of education completed, which not only has a bearing on your employability in the short run, but could hobble your earning power in the future if you cut it short for the baby. By no means quit school to get a job so you can pay the baby bills. Such a decision could fill you with unbelievable regret and resentment. It is no secret that most domestic arguments are about finances. You are going to have them. Don't add to those infuriating battles the deep resentment against wife and child because you cashed in your education for a box of diapers.

The organizations that I am going to tell you about will reinforce the idea that you must finish your education. They also realize that if you stay in school there will be extra hardship for you and your family. But school doesn't last forever, although the lack of education can dog you for the rest of your life. Those same organizations are designed to assist you through the few years when you must cope with having a baby *and* completing your education.

If you are seriously considering marriage, you owe it to yourself to evaluate your chances for success with an open mind. If you are at least eighteen years old, you have a chance to make marriage work, but not much of one. The world may be ready to put you to work by that time, but if you don't have at least the minimum amount of support from your family and your girlfriend's family, your chances are slim.

> Pregnant teenagers marry about 10 percent of the time, but the marriages tend to be short-lived. The divorce rate for parents younger than eighteen is three times greater than that for parents who have their first child after age twenty. And 44 percent of

young women who give birth between the ages of fourteen and seventeen are divorced fifteen years later.

Whatever their intentions, teenage fathers and mothers are unprepared for the responsibilities of parenthood, and their offspring often suffer negative consequences. Two percent of children born to parents younger than seventeen die before their first birthday, twice the rate for children in other American families. One reason these babies tend to have health problems is that their young mothers have poor diets and don't understand the essentials of prenatal care.

Teenage parents tend to have unrealistic expectations of their children and immature ideas about what babies are like (such as when they should begin walking or talking or become toilet trained). They may pressure their offspring to do these things before they are physically able. Sometimes this ignorance leads to impatience, intolerance, and physical abuse. Statistics show that teenage parents are more likely than more mature parents to resort to child abuse.[5]

Those are some pretty hard truths and tragic consequences regarding teenage marriage and teenage parenthood. Remember that although statistics don't lie, neither do they care. If you care, as I care, as the counselors who desire to help teen fathers care, you can defy the statistics enough to make an infinitesimal dent in the

---

[5] Robinson, Bryan, *Psychology Today*, December 1985, pp. 66–70.

statistical scorecard—ane make an enormous contribution to your soul and the souls of others, especially your child.

The hard truths contained in the passage from *Psychology Today* can be very intimidating. For the teenage father who is willing to postpone marriage, however, the article contains a good many clues that can lead him to a satisfying relationship with his child, and also the mother of that child.

The catalog of woes, from the evident unpreparedness of teenage parents, to the potential for child abuse, can be related directly to lack of experience. An obvious solution to the problem is to find somebody who has the experience to lend a hand, to commit the benefits of that experience to your baby, and to do it for free. Where do you look to find such a person? Look no further than the grandmother of that child, your girlfriend's mother.

Do not think for a minute that you are placing an unfair burden on the frail shoulders of Granny. The fact that you and the mother of your child are teenagers should indicate that Granny isn't all that old or frail. In fact, Granny would probably go upside your head with a rolling pin if you tried to exclude her from raising the infant.

We've established that more and more teenage mothers are keeping the baby. The intense pressure put upon the teenage mother by her family to keep and raise the baby is a sign of caring, even if it is the overbearing kind. That kind of family is actually a united support group that is ready and waiting to help raise your child. True, the same group may shriek at the sight of *you*, but maybe not. If the girl's family disapproves of you, it is possible to change their feelings toward you by working with them instead of against them. You should be willing to cooperate and compromise. If the thought of that makes you cringe, try thinking of the rest of your life spent without the privilege of watching your lifeblood grow.

The great advantage to such a cohesive support system is that it is an experienced one. The mother of your child was born and raised successfully, so her parents must have a pretty good idea what to do with a baby. You can avoid the catalog of hard truths, such as a baby's death from poor nutrition, difficulties caused by inexperienced prenatal care, the unrealistic expectations and immature ideas, and the potential for child abuse caused by impatience and frustration.

If you don't try to take away their daughter and their grandchild, and if you enlist their help, maybe the girl's parents will be more sympathetic to and accepting of you. That is what you want, after all. You want to be in the picture. But beware! The *Psychology Today* article continues:

> Teenage fathers who stay in the picture often face unbridled hostility from their girlfriends' families. Nine [out of 100] of our young fathers said that their girlfriends' parents didn't like or didn't speak to them. Steve, 17, tells us, "I knew I could have been much more involved in my baby's birth. But I was afraid to admit that I was the father. When people find out you're the one, they try to take you to court and hassle you. I wanted to go to the hospital with her, but I was scared that would only lead to more trouble for both of us. Anyway, her parents didn't want me hanging around at all."

Young fathers are often left in the dark when decisions are made about their babies, primarily by the mother and her parents. Teenage fathers are often not told when the baby is born or that their children have been adopted or turned over to foster care.

Once you realize that there is no guarantee that you will be given the chance to raise your child, or even lay eyes on it, possibility of cooperating with the girl's family, in exchange for their expertise and your access to the child, becomes not only appealing but a golden opportunity.

In this scenario, where you work from the outside in full cooperation with the girl's family, the hardest and most important barrier you will face is the stereotype of the teenage father.

Blame it on pride, prejudice or bitter experience, but fathers have long been the forgotten figures in teenage pregnancy. Stereotyped as insensitive and irresponsible, they are usually ignored by the numerous counseling programs run by and for females only. Now, however, those sentiments are finally beginning to recede. A growing body of research indicates that many young, unmarried fathers would willingly cherish and succor their off-spring—if they could.[6]

The last line of that passage resonates in other studies

---

[6] Langway, Lynn, *Newsweek*, 10/24/83, pp. 118.

and articles that describe the types of opposition that a teenage father faces; for instance, *Psychology Today*, June 1985, p. 66:

> With few legal rights, and usually with little income and few prospects, the more than two million unwed teenage fathers in this country have very little chance of playing an active role in their children's lives. And despite the popular stereotype of the unwed father as a love-'em-and-leave-'em family deserter, there is evidence that the majority of unwed fathers are concerned with the futures of their children.

Bryan Robinson writes in *Psychology Today* (December 1985):

> Although junior and senior high school boys are responsible for 1.1 million pregnancies in this country every year, our understanding of these men is woefully incomplete. Most people think that the teenage fathers' first impulse is to walk away from their parental responsibilities. In books and movies they are portrayed as self-centered ne'er-do-wells, interested only in sexual gratification, who have fleeting, casual relationships with their girlfriends and hit the road at the first hint of pregnancy.
>
> But our research and others' shows that many young men go through the same emotional struggle that young mothers do. These boys usually know their girlfriends for a year or more and report feelings ranging from affection to love. A growing number are choosing not to abandon their babies.

The difficulty arises when we try to find outreach programs that are as concerned about the teenage father as
he is about his baby. The existing counseling programs,
"run by and for women," often reflect the hostility gen-
erated by the girl's family and some of the stiffer pre-
cepts of radical feminism. Whatever the reason, the
hostility appears to be fueled by misconceptions and
duly misguided. Robinson writes:

> Social workers and people who provide medical
> services routinely ignore the father's feelings.
> When professionals do get the young fathers in-
> volved, many often discover an eagerness to talk
> about feelings and a desire to be involved in the
> birth. When eighteen-year-old Mike's daughter was
> born in Rawlins, Wyoming, for example, the
> fifteen-year-old mother wanted to put the baby up
> for adoption. Mike interceded, received custody of
> his child, and is now rearing her with his parents'
> help.

"Help" is the key to Mike's successful defense of his
fatherhood. He accepted help from his own family,
which he undoubtedly needed to raise a baby girl, but
more important is the fact that he took the initiative and
helped himself.

The trends toward mothers keeping the babies and
the lessening of hostility toward teenage fathers bode
well for the young men in that position. It is also
apparent that there are a lot of prickly barriers and
obstacles for the teenage father to overcome in order to
participate in the birth and growth of the child that he
fathered. Besides the legal void, the hostility, and the

shortage of assistance, there is an even greater stumbling block that the teenage father has to confront: himself. Robinson writes:

> Teenage fathers often want babies as much as teenage mothers do, for many of the same reasons. A child may be the first thing in their young lives that seems truly theirs. For those performing poorly in school, caring for a baby may be their first tangible accomplishment. For those reared in troubled homes, the infant may be the first human from whom they can receive love.

Those are strong and genuine feelings for a young man or woman to hold, and it appears that for the most part both teenage father and mother share the desire to nurture as well as the contingent anxieties. But those same anxieties seem magnified for the teenage father.

Swayed by social conditioning and trapped by the pressures of burgeoning manhood, the teenage male is convinced that an outward show of affection and emotional commitment is a sign of weakness. Add to that the overwhelming peer pressure that glorifies independence and self-sufficiency, plus popular reverence for the "strong, silent type," and the result is a set of conditions that translate the act of seeking help into an admission of failure. These conditions exist despite documented evidence that these same individuals care deeply about their infant, but

> . . . this interest is quickly dampened by the men's own inhibitions, by social pressures and by the legal system. "First of all, men don't reach out for help.

You have to reach out to them," says Sally Brown of San Francisco's Teenage Pregnancy and Parenting Project. "We have male counselors who go to basketball courts, recreation centers and street corners. The counselors know the streets, they know the families of these guys and they know where they're coming from."[7]

[7] *Psychology Today*, June 1985, p. 66.

CHAPTER 10

Tapp

Before 1983 very few programs existed in the United States for teen fathers. The Teenage Pregnancy and Parenting Project (TAPP), run by the Family Service Agency and the Unified School District of San Francisco, was originally developed to assist teenage mothers. Then Robin Jackson, a graduate of the Social Work School at the University of California at Berkeley, got a job at TAPP, thinking he would have a chance to help young fathers like himself. But he soon found that TAPP, like virtually every program like it in the country, was designed for the teen mother.

"The boys would sit in the office," said Jackson, "and sometimes they'd actually be taking care of the baby, but no one would speak to them. It was easier to work with girls—they're submissive—but the boys were tagged as bad guys. If a boy misses an appointment, they say the hell with him, but if a girl doesn't come, they go out looking for her.

As a man who had new ideas about fathering,

Jackson found himself in conflict with women who had new ideas about sisterhood. "All they had was programs for women run by women. The idea was that all men were potentially bums—and especially young guys who had got a girl pregnant."

But having grown up in the projects in Steelton (Pa.), Robin knew that each teenage father is standing on the edge of a pit. Teen fathers are among America's great losers, looked down upon by everyone. Usually they quit school and start a lifetime of menial jobs. It's not surprising that many of them soon run away—or turn to crime.

Jackson began by trying to put together a program by himself, going to boys' homes, trying to get them jobs, spending hours on the phone, to get together support groups that at first contained only one or two young fathers. When a number of foundations started looking around for agencies that could start teen fathers' programs, Jackson was more than ready for them, and the San Francisco Foundation came through with modest funds to start the program through TAPP. Within eighteen months he had put 50 boys through training.[1]

TAPP offers a wide range of services, which include support groups and courses in child care, nutrition, and shopping for age-appropriate toys. "Teen fathers are taught how to change, feed, and hold their babies. At the same time, the young men train in a trade and finish

---

[1] Larner, Jeremy, *Esquire*, December 1984, pp. 264–267.

school, increasing the likelihood that they will find a job."[2]

Albert Gasca, an eighteen-year-old father of an eighteen-month-old girl, gave up his street gang in the barrio to join TAPP's pioneering program. "I want to see my little girl grow up," says Gasca. "It's not easy coming here. Guys have too much pride to say, 'Can you help me?'"[3]

As tough as it is to get reluctant fathers to join the program, it is equally tough to change some of the preconceptions of those who do enroll. TAPP workers discovered that the expectant teenage father's primary concern is to get a job so he can support his new family.

"These young men are surrounded by a culture that says they must be walking wallets," said TAPP Project Director Amy Williams. "We have a dickens of a time convincing them that they should stay in school so that they can bring in more money later on."[4]

Education and training are passkeys to a brighter future for you and your child. Bailing out of school to earn the minimum wage at a fast-food joint may pay for tomorrow's baby formula, but it won't pay for the milk and meatloaf when baby grows teeth and a bigger appetite and you're still stuck in a dead-end job. That is why outreach programs like TAPP encourage teenage fathers to finish their education, whether it means staying in school, going back to school, or taking high school equivalency programs.

---

[2] Robinson, Bryan, *Psychology Today*, December 1985, pp. 66–70.

[3] Langway, Lynn, *Newsweek*, 10/24/83, p. 118.

[4] *Psychology Today*, June 1985, p. 66.

CHAPTER 11

Teen Fathers

Program

R on Johnson, like Robin Jackson of TAPP, suffered as a struggling young man fighting for a future. At twelve years of age Ron was rescued from a hopeless life as a member of a Brooklyn street gang by a martial arts teacher, Pedro Vialet. Pedro steered Ron into an Upward Bound program at Columbia University, where Ron eventually received an undergraduate degree in biology and then spent thirteen years as a teacher developing a rapport with kids.

Ron Johnson transferred himself to Lawndale, California, where he took a position as director of the Teen Fathers Program at the Youth and Family Center.

The center deals with every aspect of early pregnancy ...and Johnson has been responsible for persuading some forty young men to behave like the fathers they are. The program offers tutoring as well as counseling on being a parent, sex, and employment (including how to fill out a job application).

Johnson is both demanding and sympathetic. "We challenge them to do better, to hold on, be strong," he says. "And to take responsibility for themselves and their actions. We challenge them to be men. Most teenage fathers want to be with their children, but they can't support the child, and it's hard to feel good about yourself as a man if you earn only $4 to $5 an hour."[1]

Like the counselors at TAPP, Johnson has to go out and beat the bushes to find teenage fathers, who are reluctant to seek assistance. Johnson's enrollment rate is a whopping 70 percent of the teenage fathers who are approached by the Teen Fathers Program.

Teen Fathers counselors recommend that young fathers who are in school stay in school. If an individual is prepared to go to work, they will help him find a job.

Some of Ron Johnson's earthier instruction includes how to change a diaper, mix a formula, and hold a baby. "A lot of these guys pick up a child like they pick up a basketball," he says, smiling.

---

[1] Van Biema, David, *People Weekly*, 12/1/86, pp. 81–82.

The Portland
Fatherhood Project

The Portland Fatherhood Project is administered by the National Council of Jewish Women. It is supported by a Ford Foundation grant, the Oregon Community Foundation, local sources such as church groups, and volunteer help from college students and therapists. The project gives classes in prenatal and postnatal care to 125 fathers of various ethnic backgrounds each year.

The project is headed by thirty-two-year-old John Lass, who acts as teacher, confidant, counselor, and, as a father, role model.

"A lot of these guys," says Lass, "do not know what a father is supposed to do. Many of them had no fathers around." Lass concentrates first on baby care—feeding, diapering, even how to play with an infant. He also tries to help the teenagers with their futures. Since most are high school dropouts, he encourages them to get equivalency diplomas and, later, job skills training. "These fathers do not think of themselves as nurturers unless they are also providers," Lass says, "but they can be just as nurturing as the mothers."[1]

Many of the fathers enrolled in the Portland Fatherhood Project take Lamaze classes and assist in the birth. And most of these teenage fathers are steered into the program by their girlfriends.

---

[1] Mason, Janet, *Life*, June 1984, pp. 96–100.

CHAPTER 13

Other Programs

APP, Teen Fathers, and the Portland Fatherhood Project share a common ideal: they are designed specifically for the teenage father. Only TAPP's program dovetails with programs designed for the teenage mother. But the number of teen fathers who are encouraged to enroll by their girlfriends indicates that programs designed for both parents would also be successful.

Under the coordination of New York City's Bank Street College of Education, and supported by the Ford Foundation, eight experimental projects are currently striving to encourage paternal involvement in teenage parenting. The programs operate under the umbrella of the Teen Parent Collaboration.

The Portland Fatherhood Project is one of these programs. In Bridgeport, Connecticut, the Catholic Coalition and the Council on Adolescent Programs work with 50 Hispanic fathers toward the goal of paternal involvement. Philadelphia's Medical College of Pennsylvania Hospital offers coed classes in natural childbirth and bottlefeeding. The Teen Indian Parent's Program advises fathers in Minneapolis on nutrition and prevention of child abuse and teaches them how to play with their infant. The Teen Parent Collaboration also provides nutritional information, guidance in child care, and counseling in Louisville, Kentucky.

One program that specializes in postnatal care is the Michigan Association Concerned with School-aged Parents (MASCAP), in Lansing. MASCAP includes teenage fathers in its services to expectant mothers. The program provides counseling, classes in birthing techniques, and advice on family planning. At another Teen Fathers Program in Cleveland, Ohio, counselors encourage teen fathers to be more involved with their children and to become supportive of their mothers.

For younger adolescent parents, there is the Services to Young Families program of the Cuyahoga County Welfare Department in Cleveland. This program offers such services as

> ...an alternative school, medical care, individual counseling, parent education classes, summer pre-employment training, and sewing and crafts classes to pregnant teenagers age sixteen and younger. To insure their consistent attendance, transportation is provided, and meals are also an integral part of the all-day program.
>
> The program offers help and information specifically geared to young teenagers who are living with their own parents or extended family members, have several years of school yet to complete and have no immediate potential for independent living. The program recognizes their dependence and

cognitive immaturity, and materials and activities have been designed with these limitations in mind.[1]

The Maternal and Infant Care Project at Grady Hospital in Atlanta, like the services of the Young Families Program, is focused primarily on the medical and counseling needs of teenagers younger than sixteen at the time of conception. Both programs are administered by the Child Welfare League.

Project Redirection is a nationwide program for older teenagers, developed by Manpower Demonstration Research Corporation in New York City. Project Redirection directs teen parents to finish school, obtain job training, and assists with job placement.

As you can see, there has been a breakthrough in the orientation of outreach assistance programs in that the teenage father is no longer ignored and scorned. In order to benefit from these services, however, you have to take that first step toward your goal: to become an active, caring, and helpful father to your child.

To achieve that goal, the teen father has to wrestle with family outrage, unfair stereotypes, and a system of resources designed mostly for women. But there are now organizations that cater strictly to the father, and more women-directed programs are opening their services to include the teen father.

The highest hurdle is your own attitude toward yourself and your position as a teenage father. Don't isolate yourself with fear disguised as cool. Remember that it is

---

[1] Miller, Shelby, *Children Today*, May 1985, pp. 26–29.

your child who needs you the most, and your child needs you to be there, and to be aware.

> The Super Bowl macho man will break but not bend. The idea of masculinity that each [teen father] learns from the world around him is likely to ruin him as a husband and a father. Until he learns that his manhood is not at stake with every difference, he will be stuck with the sterile pride of the drunk on the corner. His sons, too, may be stuck and repeat the pattern of a father who can't hang in there with his children. The only way out is to connect. [2]

One last word of advice: If you find yourself on the verge of becoming a teen father and you want to explore your options, look in the Yellow Pages of your telephone book under Social Services for listings under Family Planning, Parenthood, Pregnancy, or Adolescent Counseling. If any of these agencies do not deal specifically with teenage fatherhood, they can certainly refer you to a program that does.

Other useful resources in this matter are your school guidance counselor and your priest, minister, or rabbi.

---

[2] Larner, Jeremy, *Esquire*, December 1984, pp. 264–267.

Bibliography

Barbera-Hogan, M. "Teen Fathers: The Other Side of the Story." *Teen* 31:32+, July 1987.

"Black Teen Fathers Not So Irresponsible." *Jet* 70-28, August 11, 1986.

Dunne, J. "A Single Father." *New York Times Magazine*, December 24, 1984.

Larner, J. "The Sins of Our Fathers." *Esquire* 102-264-7, December 1984.

Mason, J. "Bringing Up Teenage Fathers." *Life* 7:96=100+, June 1984.

"Reality of Teen Fatherhood, The." *Teen* 28:18+, November 1984.

Spink, S. "Working Part-time While in School Has Made Me Self-sufficient—and Proud of Myself." *Seventeen* 43:24, January 1984.

Van Biema, D. "Unprepared, Unwanted, and Unwed." *People Weekly* 26:81-2+, December 1986.

Index